NEW CLASSIC
COCKTAILS

For Sarah, my princess

First published in Great Britain in 2003 by
Hamlyn, a division of Octopus Publishing Group Ltd
2–4 Heron Quays, London E14 4JP

Copyright © Octopus Publishing Group Ltd 2003

All rights reserved. No part of this work may be
reproduced or utilized in any form or by any means,
electronic or mechanical, including photocopying,
recording or by any information storage and retrieval
system, without the prior written permission of
the publisher.

ISBN 0 600 60886 7

A CIP catalogue record for this book is available
from the British Library

Printed in China

10 9 8 7 6 5 4 3 2 1

hamlyn

NEW CLASSIC
COCKTAILS

EVERYONE'S FAVOURITES AND CONTEMPORARY VARIATIONS

Allan Gage

Notes for American readers

Standard level spoon measures are used in all recipes.

1 tablespoon = one 15 ml spoon
1 teaspoon = one 5 ml spoon

Imperial and metric measurements have been given in some of the recipes. Use one set of measurements only and not a mixture of both.

UK	US
caster sugar	granulated sugar
cocktail cherries	maraschino cherries
cocktail stick	toothpick
double cream	heavy cream
drinking chocolate	presweetened cocoa powder
icing sugar	confectioners' sugar
jug	pitcher
lemon rind	lemon peel or zest
single cream	light cream
soda water	club soda

Note:

The Department of Health advises that eggs should not be consumed raw. It is prudent for more vulnerable people such as pregnant and nursing mothers, invalids, the elderly, babies and young children to avoid raw eggs.

CONTENTS

Introduction

Take a classic cocktail
and give it a twist...

Contemporary ingredients, such as black and flavoured vodkas, can be used to give a new twist to classic cocktails. In this book, each classic recipe is accompanied by its modern twist, giving 160 exciting cocktails. Start by making the new versions of your old favourites, or if you are feeling adventurous, why not try recipes you've never tasted before?

Cocktail history and culture

We don't know the origin of the word 'cocktail', but we do know that people have been enjoying mixed drinks for hundreds of years, and that the first written references to cocktails appeared in the USA early in the 19th century.

The early cocktails Perhaps the earliest cocktail, the Mint Julep was first recorded in the early 1800s, followed throughout the century by a number of familiar cocktails, including the Gin Fizz, the Manhattan, the Planter's Punch and the Old Fashioned. The Dry Martini dates from 1910 and the Pink Lady from 1912 but these were drinks for the rich and fashionable – it was only with Prohibition that the cocktail acquired widespread popularity.

Prohibition Between 1920 and 1933, prohibition by US federal law of the manufacture, transportation and sale of intoxicating beverages accounted for what was called – depending on your point of view – both a 'ridiculous drought' and a 'noble experiment'. Despite its good intentions, Prohibition led to the cocktail explosion, and the 1920s and 1930s were the golden age.

Prohibition coincided with the period after the Great War when the younger generation on both sides of the Atlantic – but led by America – started freeing themselves of old social conventions. New music (the start of the Jazz Age), energetic dancing (the Charleston and the One Step), shorter skirts for women and a loosening of sexual inhibitions became the 'in thing'. With liquor in the USA now illegal, the consumption of spirits was forced underground. Combined bar/restaurant/clubs called speakeasies sprang up in the big US cities. Many were luxuriously fitted out and a far cry from the hotel and saloon bars of earlier days. Such venues were the perfect home for jazz crooners and underground drinking, and here both class and sexual boundaries broke down. Women were allowed in bars for the first time. Cocktails brought all manner of drinkers together. Made with fruit juice, cream and sweeteners to mask the rough taste of the illegally distilled low-grade liquor, cocktails were drunk by everyone, no longer just the smart. The illicit status of the cocktail only increased its appeal among ordinary drinkers and gave it an air of glamour and danger, an air enhanced by its association with gangsters like Al Capone who dominated the black market in smuggled booze.

While all this was going on in the USA, Cuba acquired a thriving international bar culture as bars sprang up to meet the demands of ferry-hopping Yanks from Florida wanting a drink. At the same time bars popped up all over Europe – such as Harry's Bars in Venice and Paris and the American Bar at the Savoy Hotel in London. These bars catered both for travelling Americans and for those Europeans who wished to imitate the glamorous, enviable lifestyle exported by Hollywood. Bartenders here had the luxury of creating cocktails using fine European spirits and liqueurs, and invented cocktails like the White Lady. By the

late 1920s, the cocktail party was an established part of the smart London social scene.

Before Prohibition, whiskey was probably the most popular spirit in the USA. But during Prohibition, distilling a neutral grain spirit that didn't require ageing was more practical, and 'bathtub' gin became the most widely available spirit of the underground cocktail culture.

Prohibition was repealed in 1933 – when the US government decided to cash in on the billions of dollars being spent on smuggled liquor. Cocktails remained – and improved with the better standard of liquor available.

After Prohibition The appeal of cocktails declined during the years of the Depression and Second World War, but reappeared with post-war prosperity among wealthier Americans. In the 1950s, vodka started to become a favourite spirit base for cocktails. Cocktail lounges came into existence and cocktail parties were the thing to do at home.

Out of fashion in the sex, drugs and rock'n'roll era of the Swinging Sixties, cocktails picked up again a decade later with fern bars – the first of which was opened in San Francisco in 1969 by Norman Hobday, aka Henry Africa. Such fern-filled bars popularized the sweet 'disco cocktails' like the Piña Colada, Harvey Wallbanger and Tequila Sunrise.

At this time in Britain, where cocktails had never regained the heights of their 1920s heyday, London's Covent Garden saw the arrival of trend-setting bars such as Peppermint Park and Café Pacifico, which introduced cocktails to a much wider audience.

In the ever-cyclical nature of fashion, cocktails became uncool again during the 1980s when the proliferation of New World wines and the wine-drinking yuppy culture saw many cocktail bars give way to wine bars.

Today's cocktails – the new classics Since the early 1990s, cocktails have become mainstream once more, appealing to cocktail connoisseurs, lounge lizards and bar flies. This trend has been driven by consumers' thirst for sophistication and helped by the US trend for 'designer martinis', so-called 'alterna-tinis', made with flavoured vodkas, and the popularity of bottled ready-to-drink cocktails.

Romantic nostalgia for the Jazz Age and for the cocktail lounges of the 1950s and 1960s has fuelled the mushrooming of theme bars and lounges modelled on the cocktail bars, lounges and supper clubs of bygone eras. Here, a whole new breed of cocktails is emerging – cocktail classics (an accolade granted to only a small number of the hundreds of cocktails around) with an interesting twist.

Constantly adapted since its inception in the 19th century, the Martini is now leading the current resurgence of interest in classic cocktails. The original 50/50 ratio of vermouth and gin has slowly changed over the years to a drink where the base spirit is just as likely to be vodka as gin and, if it is used at all, the vermouth may be just swirled around the glass or lightly spritzed into it. On the menus at today's trendy watering holes, you'll find the term 'martini' has been stretched to cover almost any cocktail served in a martini glass, with any number of variations on the original gin/vermouth combination. So-called Fruit Martinis are made with flavoured vodkas, while a Chocolate Martini relies on Cointreau and crème de cacao instead of vermouth, and might be served in a glass rimmed and decorated with chocolate.

The number of cocktails is constantly growing, thanks to increased access to exotic ingredients, the imagination of bartenders and international cocktail competitions, which constantly introduce new ideas. Yet comparatively few modern cocktail recipes last for more than a generation or so, unlike the classic cocktails which have withstood the test of time and remained popular for their subtle combinations of a limited number of ingredients.

The latest challenge for bartenders is to use the more exotic ingredients now increasingly available to provide perfect twists for the old classics. Such ingredients include ginger, lemon and lime oil, cardamom, kumquats, pink grapefruit juice, espresso syrup, kiwi fruit schnapps, lychee liqueur, watermelon schnapps and vodkas flavoured with almost anything from honey, lemon, orange, blackberry and cranberry to vanilla and red peppers.

Ingredients

A cocktail must smell good, taste great and look attractive! Its smell and taste rely on the quality of the ingredients, its appearance owes much to its colour and the multitude of decorations and garnishes available – from paper parasols, swizzle sticks, indoor sparklers and trendy straws to floating flower heads, citrus rind spirals and assorted fruits and vegetables.

Alcoholic content Most cocktails consist of a spirit base – brandy, gin, rum, vodka, whisky (whiskey in the USA and Ireland) or tequila – plus additional ingredients like liqueurs, fruit juices, fruit-flavoured syrups, cream, eggs and mixers. Liqueurs are essentially high-quality spirits flavoured with the flowers, fruits, seeds or leaves of plants and sweetened with sugar. Some of the most popular flavours today include orange (Grand Marnier, Cointreau), chocolate (crème de cacao), coffee (Kahlúa, Tia Maria), anise (Pernod) and peppermint (crème de menthe).

Fruit juices, mixers and other flavourings
Many cocktails include some sort of fruit juice. Always use the type of juice specified in the recipe – bottled and carton juices are not a substitute for freshly squeezed fruit juice. Other mixers used in cocktails include carbonated non-alcoholic drinks like cola, lemonade, soda, ginger ale and tonic. Cocktail flavourings include bitters (a powerful herbal or fruit-flavoured essence used in very small quantities), salt, Tabasco and Worcestershire sauce, as well as sweet syrups like grenadine and simple sugar syrup, which you can make yourself or buy ready-made.

Sugar syrup This may be used instead of sugar to sweeten cocktails and give them more body. It can be purchased, but is simple to make at home. Put 4 tablespoons of caster sugar and 4 tablespoons of water into a small pan and stir over a low heat until the sugar has dissolved. Bring to the boil and boil, without stirring, for 1–2 minutes. Sugar syrup can be stored in a sterilized bottle in the refrigerator for up to 2 months.

Ice Ice is essential for cocktails. Crushed ice cools a drink more effectively and more quickly than cracked ice but too much of it will dilute a drink too fast. Cracked ice is the best choice for cocktails that require blending, to save damaging the blender blades. Make your own cracked ice by hitting a strong polythene bag or a clean tea towel full of ice with a rolling pin; for crushed ice, simply smash the ice a little harder, and for longer! Ice cubes last longest of all, but should never be put in a blender – they are so solid they could damage the blades.

Decorations

Cocktails demand decorations, which can be frivolous or otherwise to suit the drink. Not only decorative, they indicate whether the drinker's tastebuds can expect a sharp, crisp cocktail (indicated by a slice of lemon or lime) or a sweet drink (hinted at by a maraschino cherry or melon ball). Garnishes can also be integral to a drink's flavour, such as the flamed orange rind in a Cosmopolitan.

Fruit and vegetables Classic decorations for cocktails include thin slices of lemon, orange or lime, sprigs of mint, maraschino cherries, green olives and cocktail onions, singly or in combination. Slices of kiwi fruit, star fruit, peach, apple, tomato, carrot and cucumber, melon balls, whole strawberries, sugar-coated cranberries, wedges of pineapple, chunks of banana and tiny blue borage flowers also look enticing. Float them on the drink, twist and skewer them with a cocktail stick or split and hang them on the side of the glass as appropriate. Small ingredients like a raisin, date, nut, polo mint, coffee bean or liqueur-soaked berry can be dropped into the bottom of clear drinks.

Fruit rind Make spirals using a canelle knife or swivel-headed vegetable peeler to pare a long thin strand of rind from a citrus fruit (lemon, lime, orange or grapefruit). Include a little pith with the zest to give it body, then wind the spiral around the handle of a wooden spoon and freeze. Drape the spiral over the cocktail glass, tie it in a decorative knot or loop it around a cherry. You can also cut the skins of apples or pears into shapes and drape over the glass for effect.

Dusting Sprinkle creamy drinks with grated nutmeg, chocolate or fresh root ginger, or with desiccated coconut, chopped nuts, crushed biscuits or chocolate chips or shavings.

Decorated rims Wet the rim of the glass with beaten egg white, a slice of citrus fruit, water or sugar syrup, then invert the glass into a saucer of fine sugar crystals, salt (for Margaritas), desiccated coconut or presweetened cocoa powder for an appealing look.

Ice Freeze single raspberries, apple chunks, flowers or sprigs of mint inside ice cubes, or freeze fruit juices to make flavoured ice cubes.

11

Terms and techniques

Blend A recipe that tells you to blend your cocktail simply means to place all your ingredients, along with ice (preferably crushed or cracked), in an electric blender or liquidizer and press the button. *Voilà!* You have a blended cocktail. Blending is necessary for cocktails that contain fresh fruit or crushed ice, such as a Frozen Margarita.

Never blend carbonated soft drinks or Champagne or your mixture will explode! Add these ingredients only after blending the other elements of the cocktail.

Build To build a drink, simply fill your glass with ice, pour in the ingredients and serve.

Float This can refer to floating a decoration or a final liquid ingredient on top of your cocktail. To get one liquid to float on top of another you need to hold the flat end of a bar spoon or an inverted teaspoon against the inside of the glass and in contact with the drink. Slowly pour the liquid over the spoon and it should settle on the surface of the drink – the success of this technique depends on the density of your liquid layers. The cream in an Irish Coffee is floated on the coffee in this way.

Frappé A cocktail, liqueur or spirit served frappé is one that is served over finely crushed ice. Green crème de menthe, decorated with a sprig of mint, for example, makes a refreshing after-dinner drink when served frappé.

Layer Also known as a pousse café, this involves floating (see left) liqueurs of different densities on top of one another in a small, slim, straight-sided glass. The three-layered B-52 is an example of a layered cocktail.

Muddle Muddling means crushing and mixing ingredients like fruits and herbs, often in the glass in which the cocktail is served. This extracts as much flavour as possible from the fresh ingredients and is usually done with a pestle-like tool called a 'muddler'. The Mint Julep and the Mojito both rely on muddling to release the full flavour of the fresh mint leaves.

On the rocks A drink served 'on the rocks' means one that is served over ice cubes – preferably a glassful of ice.

Shake Cocktails made of fruit juices, thick liqueurs, cream, milk and other ingredients that require thorough mixing are the ones that need shaking. The technique is to place everything in a cocktail shaker, together with plenty of cubed or cracked ice, which chills the drink and acts as a beater in the shaker. Holding the shaker in two hands, shake it vigorously using a quick pumping action until the outside of the shaker is frosty. Pour the cocktail into the glass, straining it (see right) as you pour if required, and serve. The rule is the same as for blended cocktails: to prevent a messy situation, never shake fizzy ingredients!

Stir The simplest of cocktail-making methods, stirring is used for clear drinks such as the Dry Martini or Tequini, whose appearance would be spoiled by vigorous shaking, and the drink would also become too diluted. Place your ingredients with ice in a mixing glass and stir gently with a long-handled bar spoon. Strain into a fresh glass and serve.

Straight up A request for 'straight up' means a drink served without ice.

Strain Cocktails often need to be strained before serving to remove ice, fragments of fruit or anything that might spoil the look of the drink. Some cocktail shakers come with their own built-in strainer, otherwise you will need to use an item that no cocktail bar can do without – a Hawthorne strainer.

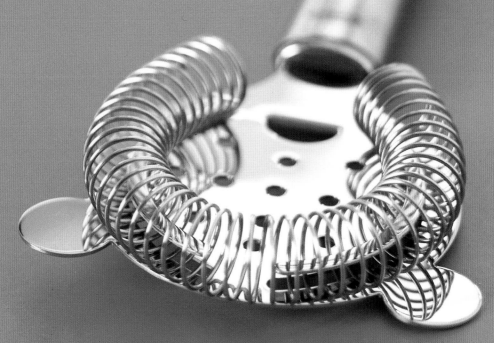

13

Glasses

The essential rule when it comes to cocktails is that they should not only taste fantastic but also look as attractive as possible. If you want to serve cocktails on a regular basis, you could get away with having just three types of glass – tall straight ones (highball or collins glasses), short straight ones (old-fashioned or rocks glasses) and traditional V-shaped cocktail or martini glasses.

Remember that cocktails are always best served in well-chilled glasses, and the chosen glass should have room for a generous measure of the drink as well as good helpings of ice and decorations.

Boston [a] Mainly used for mixing stirred drinks or shaking drinks when combined with a Boston tin, these glasses are very hard-wearing.

Cocktail/martini [b] This classic glass has a wide V-shaped bowl on a long stem. The bowl provides scope for decorating the drink and the long stem allows you to hold the glass while keeping your hot hand away from the cool drink.

Rocks [c] These glasses are often made of toughened glass – good for muddled drinks.

Hurricane [d] Shaped like a hurricane lamp, this glass is suitable for long drinks and frozen cocktails. It is probably best associated with lavish fruit decorations and a paper parasol.

Old-fashioned [e] Also called a lowball, this short sturdy tumbler is widely used for serving whisky and the Old Fashioned itself.

Highball/Collins [f] This tall tumbler is usually used for long cocktails with plenty of soda, tonic or fruit juice like the Tom Collins or Gin and Tonic. Some highball glass designs have slightly flared sides.

Coupette/Margarita [g] Similar to the cocktail glass and with similar capacity, the Margarita glass has a small bowl topped by a shallow saucer with a wide rim for the salt decoration popular with Margarita drinkers.

Shot [h] This small glass is used for potent drinks with a high alcohol content, like neat tequila or the three-layered B-52.

Sling [i] This elegant glass is perfect for long drinks such as the Russian Spring Punch.

Brandy balloon/snifter [j] The unusual shape of this large glass enables it to be cupped in the hand and swirled gently to warm the brandy and allow its aroma to be enjoyed.

Wine goblet [k] A wine goblet is perfectly suitable for almost any drink. Large ones are good for frozen drinks like a Frozen Margarita.

Champagne flute [l] Perfect for wines with fizz, the flute shape stops the bubbles disappearing too fast.

Toddy [m] The handle on the side of these glasses allows the drinker to hold hot cocktails safely and comfortably.

Champagne saucer [n] It's believed that the shallow-bowled saucer lets the Champagne bubbles disperse too quickly.

15

Moscow Mule

This drink **(right)** with 'the kick of a mule' kicked off the vodka craze in 1950s America.

6–8 cracked ice cubes
50 ml (2 fl oz) vodka
juice of 2 limes
ginger beer, to top up
lime wedges, to decorate

Put the cracked ice cubes into a highball glass. Add the vodka and lime juice, stir and top with ginger beer. Decorate with lime wedges.

Mexican Mule

*The Mexican Mule **(left)** uses gold tequila and coffee liqueur in place of the vodka for a smooth, spicy taste.*

Cut the lime into slices, put them into a highball glass and muddle with the sugar syrup. Half fill the glass with crushed ice, add the tequila and Kahlúa, stir then top up with ginger ale.

1 lime
dash of sugar syrup
  (see page 10)
crushed ice
25 ml (1 fl oz) José Cuervo
  Gold tequila
25 ml (1 fl oz) Kahlúa coffee
  liqueur
ginger ale

Sea Breeze

A long drink (left) that has changed considerably over the years. In the 1930s it was made with gin rather than vodka and with grenadine and lemon juice instead of the cranberry juice and grapefruit juice used today.

ice cubes
25 ml (1 fl oz) vodka
50 ml (2 fl oz) cranberry juice
25 ml (1 fl oz) grapefruit juice
lime wedges, to decorate

Fill a tall glass with ice cubes, pour over the vodka, cranberry juice and grapefruit juice and stir well. Decorate with lime wedges and serve with straws.

Cuban Breeze

Rum replaces the vodka in the Cuban Breeze (right) – invest in a good-quality rum for a beautifully mellow drink.

Fill a highball glass with ice cubes and add the cranberry juice. Put some ice cubes into a shaker and add the rum and grapefruit juice and shake to mix. Strain over the cranberry juice and decorate with lime wedges.

ice cubes
75 ml (3 fl oz) cranberry juice
50 ml (2 fl oz) Havana Club
  3-year-old rum
50 ml (2 fl oz) grapefruit juice
lime wedges, to decorate

Salty Dog

the classic

Traditionally a gin-based cocktail, nowadays the Salty Dog is more often made with vodka and the rim of the glass is frosted with salt (**right**). Without the salt the drink becomes a Greyhound.

orange slice

salt

6–8 ice cubes

50 ml (2 fl oz) vodka

62.5 ml (2½ fl oz)
  grapefruit juice

Moisten the rim of a glass with an orange slice then dip it in salt to coat. Put the ice cubes into the glass. Put a pinch of salt on the ice and add the vodka and grapefruit juice. Stir gently and serve.

Rising Sun

with a twist

In this drink (left), passion fruit syrup adds sweetness and an exotic tang to the classic recipe of vodka and grapefruit juice.

Put the vodka, passion fruit syrup and grapefruit juice into a shaker with ice. Shake to mix then strain into an old-fashioned glass over 6–8 ice cubes. Decorate with a pink grapefruit wheel.

50 ml (2 fl oz) vodka

2 teaspoons passion fruit syrup

75 ml (3 fl oz) grapefruit juice

ice cubes

pink grapefruit wheel, to
  decorate

21

Bloody Mary

the classic

Attributed to Harry's Bar, Paris, in 1921, this spicy mix of lemon and tomato juices, Worcestershire sauce and vodka makes a good aperitif and a great hangover cure after a heavy night **(right)**.

ice cubes
juice of ½ lemon
2 dashes Worcestershire sauce
2 dashes Tabasco (optional)
100 ml (4 fl oz) thick tomato juice
50 ml (2 fl oz) vodka
salt and ground black pepper
  (use cayenne pepper if you are
  not using Tabasco)
celery stick, to decorate

Put some ice cubes into a shaker. Add the lemon juice, Worcestershire sauce, Tabasco, if using, tomato juice and vodka. Shake well then pour into a tall glass over 4–6 ice cubes, add a pinch of salt and a pinch of pepper and decorate with a celery stick.

Plasma

with a twist

A great blend of flavours (left), including the wonderful combination of dill and Dijon mustard. The flavoured vodka gives a heavily spiced base, so add your Tabasco with care!

Put all the ingredients into a shaker with some ice cubes. Shake vigorously but briefly then strain into a highball glass over 6–8 ice cubes. Decorate with a cucumber strip and a seasoned split cherry tomato.

50 ml (2 fl oz) Absolut
  Peppar vodka
2 dashes Tabasco
4 dashes Worcestershire sauce
celery salt
black pepper
½ teaspoon Dijon mustard
1 teaspoon finely chopped dill
juice of ¼ lemon
100 ml (4 fl oz) tomato juice
ice cubes
cucumber strips and seasoned
  split cherry tomato, to decorate

23

the classic

Vodka Martini

A Vodka Martini **(left)** is the classic alternative to the gin-based Dry Martini. It is sometimes known as a Kangaroo.

5 ice cubes
7.5 ml (¼ fl oz) dry vermouth
75 ml (3 fl oz) vodka
green olive or lemon rind,
** to decorate**

Put the ice cubes into a mixing glass. Pour the vermouth over the ice and stir to coat. Discard any excess vermouth, leaving the flavoured ice. Pour the vodka over the ice and stir vigorously. Strain the drink into a chilled cocktail glass and decorate with a green olive or lemon rind.

with a twist

Vanilla Skyy

*A fruitier drink than the Vodka Martini, with hints of apple and vanilla **(right)**. Skyy is an American vodka of exceptional purity.*

Fill a mixing glass with ice cubes. Add the vermouth, stir and strain, discarding the excess vermouth and leaving the flavoured ice. Add the two vodkas and the schnapps, stir then strain into a chilled cocktail glass. Decorate with an apple chunk ice cube.

ice cubes
2 teaspoons dry vermouth
25 ml (1 fl oz) vanilla-infused
** vodka (e.g. Stoli Vanil)**
25 ml (1 fl oz) Skyy vodka
12.5 ml (½ fl oz) apple
** schnapps**
apple chunks frozen in apple
** juice in an ice cube tray,**
** to decorate**

Cosmopolitan

A pink drink, but not a girlie one, this 1990s American cocktail **(left)** is related to the Cape Codder (see page 32). Most modern recipes use flavoured vodkas such as lemon or orange. The Rude Cosmopolitan is made with tequila instead of vodka. You will need a long taper to ignite the orange oil.

25 ml (1 fl oz) vodka
12.5 ml (½ fl oz) Cointreau
25 ml (1 fl oz) cranberry juice
juice of ½ lime
ice cubes
orange twist

Put the vodka, Cointreau, cranberry juice and lime juice into a shaker. Add some ice cubes and shake until well mixed then strain into a cocktail glass. Light the taper. Holding the skin side of the orange twist away from you, squeeze the oils from the orange skin over the flame and over the surface of the drink, then drop it in.

Ginger Tom

*This warming variation **(right)** has dominant oriental flavours. Fresh lime and ginger make every sip a treat, and although the alcohol content is high, the drink slips down with ease.*

Put the gin, Cointreau, lime juice, ginger syrup, cranberry juice and some ice cubes into a shaker and shake to mix. Strain into a chilled cocktail glass and decorate with a lime twist.

37.5 ml (1½ fl oz) gin
25 ml (1 fl oz) Cointreau
dash of fresh lime juice
dash of sweetened ginger syrup
37.5 ml (1½ fl oz) cranberry juice
ice cubes
lime rind spiral, to decorate

27

Black Russian

A Black Russian (left) is a short drink made with vodka and a coffee-flavoured liqueur. It was very popular in the 1950s.

4–6 cracked ice cubes
50 ml (2 fl oz) vodka
25 ml (1 fl oz) Kahlúa
  coffee liqueur

Put the cracked ice cubes into a short glass. Add the vodka and Kahlúa and stir to mix.

Dark Knight

A luxuriously rich cocktail (right) that would make the perfect end to a sophisticated meal.

Put the Kahlúa, vodka, espresso and sugar syrup into a shaker with some ice cubes and shake to mix. Strain into a chilled martini glass and serve.

25 ml (1 fl oz) Kahlúa coffee
  liqueur
25 ml (1 fl oz) vodka
25 ml (1 fl oz) espresso coffee
2 teaspoons sugar syrup
  (see page 10)
ice cubes

White Russian

A White Russian (**left**) is similar to a Black Russian but with the addition of milk or cream. It makes an excellent after-dinner drink.

ice cubes
25 ml (1 fl oz) vodka
25 ml (1 fl oz) Kahlúa
  coffee liqueur
25 ml (1 fl oz) milk or
  double cream

Put some ice into a shaker and add the vodka, Kahlúa and milk or double cream. Shake until a frost forms on the outside of the shaker. Fill an old-fashioned glass with ice and strain the cocktail over it.

Red Star Alexander

The dark crème de cacao and nutmeg garnish give a deliciously rich twist (right) to the classic white russian.

Put the vodka, Kahlúa, dark crème de cacao, cream and some ice into a shaker and shake to mix. Strain into a chilled cocktail glass and sprinkle with nutmeg.

25 ml (1 fl oz) vodka
25 ml (1 fl oz) Kahlúa
  coffee liqueur
25 ml (1 fl oz) dark crème
  de cacao
25 ml (1 fl oz) single cream
ice
grated nutmeg, to decorate

Cape Codder

A long drink **(left)** similar to the Sea Breeze (see page 18) and one of today's most popular cocktails, thanks to the current vogue for cranberry juice. Cape Cod in Massachusetts is responsible for much of the USA's cranberry production.

ice cubes
50 ml (2 fl oz) vodka
100 ml (4 fl oz) cranberry juice
6 lime wedges

Fill a highball glass with ice cubes, add the vodka and cranberry juice, then squeeze 3 of the lime wedges into the drink. Stir well, decorate with the remaining lime wedges and serve with a straw, if you like.

Storm at Sea

A dramatic-looking concoction (right), the Blavod floats on top of the cranberry juice. Stir while drinking to ensure the flavours mix together.

Put the cranberry juice, pineapple juice and elderflower cordial into a shaker with half the ice cubes and shake to mix, then strain into an old-fashioned glass over the remaining ice cubes. Slowly add the vodka – it will separate briefly. Serve immediately.

50 ml (2 fl oz) cranberry juice
25 ml (1 fl oz) pineapple juice
2 teaspoons elderflower cordial
8–10 ice cubes
37.5 ml (1½ fl oz) Blavod vodka

the classic

Harvey Wallbanger

A popular cocktail from the 1960s **(left)** supposedly named after a Californian surfer called Harvey who drank so many Screwdrivers topped with Galliano (the Italian herb liqueur) that as he left the bar he banged and bounced from one wall to the other.

ice cubes
25 ml (1 fl oz) vodka
75 ml (3 fl oz) orange juice
1 teaspoon Galliano
orange slices, to decorate

Put some ice cubes into a shaker, and pour in the vodka and orange juice. Shake well for about 10 seconds, then strain into a highball glass filled with ice. Float the Galliano on top. Decorate with orange slices.

with a twist

Murray Hearn

*An extra boost of orange from the Cointreau and the addition of single cream make this smooth variation **(right)** all too drinkable.*

Put some ice cubes into a shaker and add the vodka, orange juice, Galliano, Cointreau and single cream. Strain into a highball glass filled with ice cubes. Decorate with an orange wheel and serve with straws, if you like.

ice cubes
37.5 ml (1½ fl oz) vodka
75 ml (3 fl oz) orange juice
12.5 ml (½ fl oz) Galliano
12.5 ml (½ fl oz) Cointreau
25 ml (1 fl oz) single cream
orange wheel, to decorate

Sex on the Beach

A long drink (left) made with vodka, fruit juices and peach schnapps, a strong dry spirit produced by the distillation of peaches.

ice cubes
25 ml (1 fl oz) vodka
25 ml (1 fl oz) peach schnapps
25 ml (1 fl oz) cranberry juice
25 ml (1 fl oz) orange juice
25 ml (1 fl oz) pineapple juice
  (optional)
orange and lime slices,
  to decorate

Put some ice into a shaker and add the vodka, peach schnapps, cranberry juice, orange juice and pineapple juice, if using, and shake well. Pour into a tall glass over 3–4 ice cubes, decorate with the orange and lime slices and serve with straws.

Sex in the Dunes

A shorter drink (right) with less juice and more kick. The raspberry and honey flavour of the Chambord combines beautifully with the peach and pineapple.

Put the vodka, schnapps, Chambord and pineapple juice into a shaker with some ice cubes and shake until the outside of the shaker becomes frosted. Strain into an old-fashioned glass filled with ice. Decorate with pineapple strips.

25 ml (1 fl oz) vodka
25 ml (1 fl oz) peach schnapps
12.5 ml ($\frac{1}{2}$ fl oz) Chambord
  liqueur
25 ml (1 fl oz) pineapple juice
ice cubes
pineapple strips, to decorate

37

the classic

Gin and Tonic

An all-time classic **(left)** which, thanks to the quinine originally included in tonic water, was particularly popular in Britain's tropical colonies as an anti-malarial medicine.

ice cubes
50 ml (2 fl oz) gin
100 ml (4 fl oz) tonic water
2 lime wedges, to decorate

Fill a highball glass with ice cubes and pour in the gin and then the tonic. Decorate with the lime wedges.

with a twist

Tanqstream

Tanqueray gin, used in this drink (right), is made in London using a recipe created by Charles Tanqueray. It is renowned for its smooth, lingering taste.

Put the gin and lime juice into a shaker with some cracked ice and shake to mix. Strain into a highball glass half-filled with cracked ice. For a dry Tanqstream, add soda water; for a less dry drink, add tonic water. Stir in the cassis and decorate with the lime wheels and fresh berries.

50 ml (2 fl oz) Tanqueray gin
2 teaspoons fresh lime juice
cracked ice
75 ml (3 fl oz) soda water or
  tonic water
2 teaspoons crème de cassis
lime wheels and fresh berries,
  to decorate

the classic Negroni

The story goes that this cocktail (left) was created during the Second World War for an American GI stationed in Italy called Negroni. He wanted an extra kick to his Americano cocktail, so the bartender added a slug of gin.

25 ml (1 fl oz) Plymouth gin
25 ml (1 fl oz) Campari
25 ml (1 fl oz) red vermouth
ice cubes
soda water to top up (optional)
orange slices, to decorate

Put the gin, Campari and vermouth into a shaker with some ice cubes and stir to mix. Strain into an old-fashioned glass filled with ice cubes and top up with soda water, if you like, and decorate with the orange slices.

with a twist *Bitter Sweet Symphony*

The sweetness of the passion fruit syrup and the bitter note of lemon juice make a drink with a great balance of flavours (right).

Put the gin, Campari, passion fruit syrup and lemon juice into a shaker with some ice cubes and shake to mix. Strain into an old-fashioned glass over 4–6 ice cubes and decorate with lemon slices.

25 ml (1 fl oz) gin
25 ml (1 fl oz) Campari
12.5 ml (½ fl oz) passion fruit syrup
12.5 ml (½ fl oz) fresh lemon juice
ice cubes
lemon slices, to decorate

White Lady

Created by Harry MacElhone in 1919 in London. Ten years later, he altered the original recipe by using gin instead of white crème de menthe, to create the White Lady we know today **(left)**.

3–4 ice cubes
50 ml (2 fl oz) gin
25 ml (1 fl oz) Cointreau
1 teaspoon fresh lemon juice
about ½ teaspoon egg white

Place the ice cubes, gin, Cointreau, lemon juice and egg white in a shaker. Shake to mix then strain into a chilled cocktail glass.

Lady of Leisure

*Chambord adds a pretty pink hue and combines with the pineapple juice to make a smoother drink with subtle berry notes **(right)**.*

Put the gin, Chambord, Cointreau, lemon juice and pineapple juice into a shaker with some ice cubes and shake to mix. Strain into a chilled cocktail glass and decorate with the orange rind.

25 ml (1 fl oz) gin
12.5 ml (½ fl oz) Chambord
  liqueur
12.5 ml (½ fl oz) Cointreau
dash of fresh lemon juice
25 ml (1 fl oz) pineapple juice
ice cubes
strips of orange rind,
  to decorate

French 75

An effervescent drink **(right)** invented during the First World War and named after a large artillery gun used by the French in trench warfare. It was originally made with brandy instead of gin.

25 ml (1 fl oz) gin
juice of ½ lemon
1 teaspoon caster sugar
chilled Champagne, to top up
lemon twist, to decorate

Put the gin, lemon juice and sugar in a Champagne flute and stir well until the sugar is dissolved. Top up with chilled Champagne and serve with a lemon twist.

French 66

Sloe gin is made by flavouring gin with sugar and sloes, hedgerow fruits rather like tiny bitter plums. It is a rich and fruity addition to this drink (left).

Soak the sugar in the bitters then drop it into a champagne flute. Add the sloe gin and lemon juice and stir. Top up with chilled Champagne and decorate with the lemon rind.

1 white sugar cube
6 dashes of orange bitters
25 ml (1 fl oz) sloe gin
juice of ¼ lemon
chilled Champagne, to top up
strip of lemon rind, to decorate

Aviation

A classic cocktail **(right)** that relies on true Maraschino, a sweet clear liqueur made from black cherries and totally different from the red chemical syrup found in jars of cocktail cherries.

62.5 ml (2½ fl oz) Plymouth gin
37.5 ml (1½ fl oz) fresh
  lemon juice
12.5 ml (½ fl oz) Maraschino
  liqueur
large dash sugar syrup
  (see page 10)
ice cubes
lemon rind, to decorate

Put the gin, lemon juice and Maraschino into a shaker, add the sugar syrup and some ice cubes and shake to mix. Strain into a chilled cocktail glass and decorate with lemon rind.

Papa's Flight

*This variation **(left)** uses lime and grapefruit juices instead of lemon, for a more complex flavour. Pink grapefruit has a sweeter flavour than the ordinary variety, and works better with gin.*

Put the gin, Maraschino, grapefruit juice, lime juice, sugar syrup and some ice cubes into a shaker and shake to mix. Strain into a chilled cocktail glass and decorate with orange rind.

50 ml (2 fl oz) gin
2 teaspoons Maraschino liqueur
25 ml (1 fl oz) grapefruit juice
dash of fresh lime juice
dash of sugar syrup
  (see page 10)
ice cubes
orange rind, to decorate

Bronx

An early 20th-century classic **(right)** believed to have been invented at the Waldorf-Astoria in New York and named by the bartender following a visit to the Bronx Zoo. It was probably the first cocktail to use a juice other than lemon or lime.

cracked ice cubes
25 ml (1 fl oz) gin
25 ml (1 fl oz) sweet vermouth
25 ml (1 fl oz) dry vermouth
50 ml (2 fl oz) orange juice
5–6 ice cubes
orange slices, to decorate

Place some cracked ice, the gin, sweet and dry vermouths and orange juice in a shaker and shake to mix. Put the ice cubes into an old-fashioned glass and strain the cocktail into it. Decorate with orange slices.

with a twist *Broadhurst Drive-by*

*Apple juice makes for a cleaner-tasting, more refreshing drink **(left)**, and the dash of lime juice adds extra zing.*

Put the gin, vermouth, lime juice and apple juice into a shaker with some ice cubes and shake to mix. Strain into a cocktail glass and decorate with a green apple slice and a cherry.

37.5 ml (1½ fl oz) gin
25 ml (1 fl oz) sweet vermouth
dash of fresh lime juice
25 ml (1 fl oz) apple juice
ice cubes
green apple slice and cocktail cherry, to decorate

49

Gimlet

Named after the handtool used to tap barrels before spirits and wines were sold in bottles, this is an old favourite of the British Navy **(left)**.

50 ml (2 fl oz) Plymouth gin
25 ml (1 fl oz) Rose's lime
 juice cordial
12.5 ml (½ fl oz) water (optional)
ice cubes
split lime wedge, to decorate

Put the gin, lime juice cordial and water, if using, into a mixing glass with some ice cubes and stir well. Strain into a cocktail glass and decorate with the lime wedge.

Blossom

The blackcurrant flavour of Absolut Kurant adds depth of flavour to this fresh-tasting variation on the classic (right).

Put the vodka, lime juice, lime juice cordial and cold water into a shaker with some ice cubes. Shake well then strain into a chilled cocktail glass. Squeeze the lime wedge into the drink then drop it in.

50 ml (2 fl oz) Absolut
 Kurant vodka
dash of fresh lime juice
dash of lime juice cordial
dash of cold water
ice cubes
lime wedge

Clover Club

the classic

An almost forgotten once-classic cocktail **(left)**, probably invented in the early 20th century, and possibly named after the Clover Club, a Philadelphia dining club started in 1881.

ice cubes
juice of 1 lime
½ teaspoon sugar syrup
  (see page 10)
1 egg white
75 ml (3 fl oz) gin
grated lime zest and lime
  wedge, to decorate

Put some ice cubes into a shaker. Pour the lime juice, sugar syrup, egg white and gin over the ice and shake to mix. Put 5 or 6 ice cubes in a rocks glass, and strain the cocktail into it. Serve decorated with grated lime zest and a lime wedge.

By Invitation Only

with a twist

*Crème de mure is a fruit liqueur flavoured with blackberries, which adds plenty to the original but doesn't detract from the classic foundations of gin and citrus in this delicious twist **(right)**.*

Put the gin, sugar syrup, lime juice and egg white into a shaker and shake to mix. Strain into a highball glass filled with ice cubes and lace with crème de mure. Decorate with 2 blackberries.

75 ml (3 fl oz) gin
2 teaspoons sugar syrup
  (see page 10)
2 teaspoons fresh lime juice
1 egg white
ice cubes
1 tablespoon crème de mure
2 blackberries, to decorate

Dry Martini

There are whole books debating the origin of this drink (left) and its authentic recipe, as well as whether it should be shaken (some say this bruises the gin) or stirred. The first Martini was probably created in the late 19th century and originally contained more sweet vermouth than gin. Much has changed since then! When you mix a Dry Martini, always ask the drinker to specify how dry he wants his drink; if the answer is 'very dry' cut down on the vermouth, if it is 'wet' increase the vermouth (this is the more traditional method).

ice cubes
12.5 ml (½ fl oz) dry vermouth
75 ml (3 fl oz) gin
green olive, to decorate

Put the ice cubes into a mixing glass. Pour the vermouth and gin over the ice and stir (never shake) vigorously and evenly without splashing, then strain into a chilled cocktail glass. Serve with a green olive on a cocktail stick.

The Doobs Martini

A complex character for the gin lover. The flavour of sloes and a hint of dry orange give this drink (right) a delicious aftertaste with great length.

Put some ice cubes into a shaker. Add the vermouth and shake well, then strain away the excess. Add the gin, sloe gin and bitters, stir, then strain into a chilled cocktail glass. Decorate with an orange twist.

ice cubes
2 teaspoons dry vermouth
50 ml (2 fl oz) gin
25 ml (1 fl oz) sloe gin
4 dashes orange bitters
orange twist, to decorate

Gin Fizz

Created in the mid-19th century, fizzes are long, gently sparkling drinks, traditionally made with a spirit, lemon juice and sugar and topped up with a fizzy drink such as soda or ginger ale. The egg white in this version **(left)** gives it an appealing frothy head.

50 ml (2 fl oz) Plymouth gin
25 ml (1 fl oz) fresh lemon juice
2–3 dashes sugar syrup
  (see page 10)
¼ beaten egg white
ice cubes
soda water
lemon wheels and mint sprig,
  to decorate

Put the gin, lemon juice, sugar syrup and egg white into a shaker with the ice cubes and shake to mix. Strain into a highball glass and top up with soda water. Decorate with lemon wheels and a mint sprig.

Sloe-ho

*This simple twist on the classic **(right)** is a beautifully coloured drink with a smooth, decadent flavour.*

Put the sloe gin, lemon juice, sugar syrup and egg white into a shaker and mix well. Strain into a highball glass filled with ice and top up with soda water. Decorate with a long spiral of lemon rind.

50 ml (2 fl oz) sloe gin
25 ml (1 fl oz) fresh lemon juice
12.5 ml (½ fl oz) sugar syrup
12.5 ml (½ fl oz) egg white
ice cubes
soda water
rind of 1 lemon, to decorate

Tom Collins

The best known of the Collinses, a group of long drinks first popular during the First World War and served in a highball or Collins glass. Originally the Tom Collins **(right)** was made with Old Tom, a slightly sweetened gin, but now it is made with dry gin.

50 ml (2 fl oz) gin
1½ teaspoons lemon juice
1 teaspoon sugar syrup
  (see page 10)
ice cubes
soda water, to top up
lemon wheel, to decorate

Put the gin, lemon juice and sugar syrup into a tall glass, stir well and fill the glass with ice. Top up with soda water and decorate with a lemon wheel.

Berry Collins

*The fresh summer fruits muddled in this drink **(left)** add an exotic flavour to the classic, making it the perfect cocktail for a long, sunny afternoon.*

Muddle the berries and strawberry syrup in the bottom of a highball glass then fill the glass with crushed ice. Add the gin, lemon juice and sugar syrup. Stir well then top up with soda water. Decorate with raspberries, blueberries and a lemon slice.

4 raspberries
4 blueberries
dash of strawberry syrup
crushed ice
50 ml (2 fl oz) gin
2 teaspoons fresh lemon juice
sugar syrup, to taste
  (see page 10)
soda water
**raspberries, blueberries and a
  lemon slice, to decorate**

59

Tequila Sunrise

the classic

This drink **(right)** is one of the cocktails that was popular during Prohibition, when the orange juice helped to disguise the taste of the raw alcohol.

50 ml (2 fl oz) tequila
100 ml (4 fl oz) orange juice
ice cubes
2 teaspoons grenadine
orange slices, to decorate

Put the tequila and orange juice into a shaker with some ice cubes and shake to mix. Fill a highball glass with ice cubes and strain the tequila mixture into it. Slowly pour in the grenadine and allow it to settle. Decorate with an orange wheel.

South for the Summer

with a twist

*A frozen blend with fresh pineapple, this refreshing cocktail **(left)** belongs on the beach at sunset.*

Drop the grenadine into a highball glass. Put the tequila, orange juice and pineapple chunks into a blender with some crushed ice and blend until slushy. Pour the mixture over the grenadine, decorate with a pineapple leaf and an orange twist and stir just before serving.

2 teaspoons grenadine
50 ml (2 fl oz) tequila
75 ml (3 fl oz) orange juice
4 fresh pineapple chunks
crushed ice
pineapple leaf and orange rind,
  to decorate

the classic

Original Margarita

Thought to date to around the 1930s or '40s, this is another cocktail with disputed origins, although there is no doubt about the ingredients – tequila, Cointreau and freshly squeezed lime juice **(right)**.

lime wedge

coarse sea salt

37.5 ml (1½ fl oz) tequila

20 ml (¾ fl oz) Cointreau

**37.5 ml (1½ fl oz) fresh
  lime juice**

ice cubes

lime wheel, to decorate

Dampen the rim of a chilled margarita glass with a lime wedge then dip the rim into the salt. Pour the tequila, Cointreau and lime juice into a shaker. Add some ice cubes and shake vigorously for about 10 seconds. Strain the cocktail into the chilled glass and decorate with a lime wheel.

with a twist

Passion Fruit Margarita

Twists on the traditional Margarita work wonderfully with powerfully flavoured fruit. This one **(left)** uses the exotic tang of passion fruit.

Moisten the rim of a margarita glass with a lime wedge and dip it in salt. Put the tequila, Cointreau, passion fruit syrup, lime juice and half the passion fruit flesh and seeds into a shaker with some ice and shake well then double-strain into a margarita glass. Add the remaining passion fruit flesh and decorate with lime wedges.

lime wedge

coarse sea salt

37.5 ml (1½ fl oz) gold tequila

25 ml (1 fl oz) Cointreau

1 teaspoon passion fruit syrup

25 ml (1 fl oz) fresh lime juice

**flesh and seeds of 1 passion
  fruit**

ice cubes

lime wedges, to decorate

Frozen Margarita

A drink **(left)** made by blending the ingredients for a traditional Margarita (see page 62) with some crushed ice.

37.5 ml (1½ fl oz) gold tequila
25 ml (1 fl oz) Cointreau
37.5 ml (1½ fl oz) fresh
  lime juice
crushed ice
lime wheel, to decorate

Put the tequila, Cointreau and lime juice into a blender with some crushed ice and blend until slushy. Pour into a large coupette and decorate with a lime wheel.

Pale Original

Ginger syrup and guava juice make a fantastic combination in this drink **(right)**, *their sweetness balanced by the lime juice.*

Put the tequila, lime juice, ginger syrup and guava juice into a blender with some crushed ice and blend until slushy. Pour into a large coupette and decorate with grated lime zest.

50 ml (2 fl oz) gold tequila
25 ml (1 fl oz) fresh lime juice
2 teaspoons ginger syrup
25 ml (1 fl oz) guava juice
crushed ice
grated lime zest, to decorate

Silk Stocking

the classic

This is everything that you expect from a sophisticated cocktail – it is smooth, unusual, beautiful to look at and deceptively powerful **(right)**.

cocoa powder
20 ml (¾ fl oz) tequila
20 ml (¾ fl oz) white crème
  de cacao
100 ml (4 fl oz) single cream
2 teaspoons grenadine
4–5 ice cubes

Dampen the rim of a chilled cocktail glass and dip it into the cocoa powder. Pour the tequila, white crème de cacao, cream and grenadine into a cocktail shaker and add the ice cubes. Shake vigorously for 10 seconds then strain into the chilled cocktail glass.

Thigh High

with a twist

This rich combination of strawberries, cream and chocolate, with a shot of tequila (left), is a taste well worth acquiring!

Muddle the strawberries and strawberry syrup in a shaker. Add the tequila, crème de cacao, single cream and ice cubes and shake to mix. Strain into a large, chilled cocktail glass and decorate with a strawberry dipped in cocoa powder.

3 strawberries
1 teaspoon strawberry syrup
25 ml (1 fl oz) tequila
25 ml (1 fl oz) dark crème
  de cacao
37.5 ml (1½ fl oz) single cream
4–5 ice cubes
1 strawberry dipped in cocoa
  powder, to decorate

the classic Tequini

This drink **(left)** is the Mexican equivalent of a Martini, with tequila replacing the gin and the orange bitters adding an exotic tang. It is one of the few drinks decorated with black rather than green olives.

ice cubes

3 dashes of orange bitters

75 ml (3 fl oz) tequila

2 teaspoons dry French vermouth, preferably Noilly Prat

3 black olives, to decorate

Fill a mixing glass with ice cubes then add the orange bitters and tequila. Stir gently with a bar spoon for 10 seconds. Take a chilled cocktail glass and add the vermouth, film the inside of the glass with the vermouth then tip it out. Stir the bitters and tequila for a further 10 seconds then strain into the chilled glass. Decorate with 3 large black olives.

with a twist *Dirty Sanchez*

*A more savoury drink **(right)** using brine instead of orange bitters, which adds a salty tang.*

Fill a mixing glass with ice cubes and add the vermouth. Stir to coat the ice, then discard the excess vermouth. Add the tequila and brine and stir until they are thoroughly chilled. Strain into a chilled cocktail glass and decorate with 2 black olives.

ice cubes

2 teaspoons Noilly Prat dry French vermouth

50 ml (2 fl oz) gold tequila (preferably Anejo)

2 teaspoons brine from a jar of black olives

2 black olives, to decorate

Tijuana Sling

A long drink **(left)** with an intriguing mixture of flavours – tequila, blackcurrant, lime and ginger.

32.5 ml (1¾ fl oz) tequila
20 ml (¾ fl oz) crème de cassis
20 ml (¾ fl oz) fresh lime juice
2 dashes Peychaud's bitters
4–5 ice cubes
100 ml (4 fl oz) ginger ale
lime wheels and blueberries,
** to decorate**

Pour the tequila, crème de cassis, lime juice and bitters into a shaker. Add some ice cubes and shake vigorously. Pour into a highball glass then top up with ginger ale. Decorate with lime wheels and blueberries.

Border Crossing

*In this twist **(right)** the addition of honey and orange bitters perfectly complements the warm tones of the ginger.*

Put the tequila, lime juice, honey and orange bitters in a shaker with some ice cubes and shake well. Pour into a highball glass and top up with ginger ale. Decorate with blueberries and lime wedges.

37.5 ml (1½ fl oz) gold tequila
25 ml (1 fl oz) fresh lime juice
25 ml (1 fl oz) clear honey
4 dashes of orange bitters
ice cubes
75 ml (3 fl oz) ginger ale
blueberries and lime wedges,
** to decorate**

Acapulco

This Caribbean cocktail **(right)** has exotic flavours of white rum, pineapple and coconut.

ice cubes
25 ml (1 fl oz) tequila
25 ml (1 fl oz) white rum
50 ml (2 fl oz) pineapple juice
25 ml (1 fl oz) grapefruit juice
25 ml (1 fl oz) coconut milk

Put some crushed ice into a shaker and pour in the tequila, rum, pineapple juice, grapefruit juice and coconut milk. Shake to mix, then pour into a hurricane glass. Serve with straws.

Off-shore

A sweet, frozen blend of rum and tequila, flavoured with sweet pineapple and refreshing mint, and wickedly laced with cream (left).

Put the rum, tequila, mint leaves, pineapple chunks, pineapple juice and single cream in a blender with some crushed ice and blend until slushy. Transfer to a hurricane glass and decorate with mint sprigs.

25 ml (1 fl oz) white rum
25 ml (1 fl oz) gold tequila
6 mint leaves
2 pineapple chunks
75 ml (3 fl oz) pineapple juice
25 ml (1 fl oz) single cream
crushed ice
mint sprigs, to decorate

Tequila Slammer

Tequila is often drunk as a slammer, and this is the original, glamorous version **(left).**

25 ml (1 fl oz) gold tequila
25 ml (1 fl oz) Champagne

Pour the tequila into a shot glass. Slowly top up with Champagne. Cover the top of the glass with the palm of your hand to seal the contents inside and grip it with your fingers. Briskly pick up the glass and slam it down on to a surface to make the drink fizz then quickly gulp it down in one, while it is still fizzing.

RAFF

A heady combination of vodka and bitter lemon, guaranteed to liven you up in no time (right)!

Pour the vodka into a tumbler, then pour in the bitter lemon. Cover the top of the glass with the palm of your hand to seal the contents inside and grip it with your fingers. Slam it down on a surface three times, then gulp it down.

25 ml (1 fl oz) vodka
25 ml (1 fl oz) bitter lemon

Brandy Alexander

A sweet and creamy after-dinner cocktail with a chocolate aftertaste **(right)**. It was originally made with gin instead of brandy and called simply an Alexander. Use ice cream instead of cream, blend well, and you have a Frozen Alexander.

25 ml (1 fl oz) brandy
25 ml (1 fl oz) brown crème
 de cacao
25 ml (1 fl oz) single cream
3 cracked ice cubes
cocoa powder

Put the brandy, crème de cacao and single cream into a shaker with the ice cubes and shake well. Strain into a chilled cocktail glass and sprinkle with cocoa powder.

Jaffa

Mandarine Napoléon is a brandy flavoured with oranges. With the addition of orange bitters, this cocktail (left) is a great balance of chocolate and orange.

Put the brandy, crème de cacao, single cream, Mandarine Napoléon and orange bitters into a shaker with some ice cubes and shake well. Strain into a chilled cocktail glass and decorate with orange-flavoured chocolate shavings.

25 ml (1 fl oz) brandy
25 ml (1 fl oz) dark crème
 de cacao
25 ml (1 fl oz) single cream
12.5 ml (½ fl oz) Mandarine
 Napoléon
2 dashes orange bitters
ice cubes
orange-flavoured chocolate
 shavings, to decorate

77

Stinger

An after-dinner cocktail **(right)** claimed by the writer Evelyn Waugh as his signature drink.

50 ml (2 fl oz) brandy
25 ml (1 fl oz) white crème de menthe
3 ice cubes
mint sprig, to decorate

Put all the ingredients into a shaker and shake well. Strain into a chilled cocktail glass and decorate with a mint sprig.

Avondale Habit

*This intriguing mix of flavours **(left)** – strawberry, mint and black pepper – is unusual but complementary, bringing out the herbal quality of the brandy that is so often ignored.*

Muddle the strawberries, sugar syrup and mint leaves in an old-fashioned glass. Almost fill the glass with crushed ice, then add the brandy and cracked pepper. Stir and add more crushed ice then lace the drink with crème de menthe. Decorate with a mint sprig and half a strawberry.

3 strawberries
dash of sugar syrup (see page 10)
4 mint leaves
crushed ice
37.5 ml (1½ fl oz) brandy
freshly cracked black pepper
2 teaspoons crème de menthe
mint sprig and strawberry half, to decorate

79

Corpse Reviver

With two brandies in its make-up, this is a powerful 'hair-of-the-dog' solution for a hangover **(left)**.

3 cracked ice cubes
50 ml (2 fl oz) brandy
25 ml (1 fl oz) Calvados
25 ml (1 fl oz) sweet vermouth
apple slices, to decorate

Put the ice, brandy, Calvados and sweet vermouth into a shaker and shake well. Strain into a chilled cocktail glass and decorate with apple slices.

Nice Pear

*Poire William subtly changes the underlying flavour of the classic from apple to pear, with gorgeous results **(right)**.*

Put the brandy, Poire William and vermouth into a shaker with some ice cubes and mix well. Strain into a chilled cocktail glass and decorate with the pear slices.

50 ml (2 fl oz) brandy
25 ml (1 fl oz) Poire William
25 ml (1 fl oz) sweet vermouth
ice cubes
skinless pear slices,
 to decorate

81

Brandy Flip

A flip is a spirit or wine shaken with egg and sugar until frothy, then dusted with nutmeg. This version **(left)** uses brandy but port, rum, sherry or whisky can be used. Early flips were warmed by plunging a red-hot poker called a 'flip-iron' into the drink just before serving.

ice cubes

1 egg

50 ml (2 fl oz) brandy

1½ teaspoons caster sugar

grated nutmeg, to decorate

Put the ice, egg, brandy and sugar into a shaker. Shake well, strain into a brandy balloon and sprinkle a little grated nutmeg on top.

The Pudding Cocktail

A rich, creamy apple-flavoured drink, The Pudding Cocktail (right) is dusted with cinnamon for a warm, spicy note.

Put the Calvados, brandy, egg yolk and caster sugar into a shaker with some ice cubes and shake until well mixed. Strain into a chilled cocktail glass. Light a long taper, hold it over the glass and sprinkle cinnamon through the flame on to the surface of the drink.

25 ml (1 fl oz) Calvados

37.5 ml (1½ fl oz) brandy

1 egg yolk

1 teaspoon caster sugar

ice cubes

ground cinnamon, to decorate

Brandy Sidecar

This classic cocktail **(right)** is thought to have been created at the Ritz Hotel in Paris during the First World War for one of the bar's regulars, an army captain who travelled in a motorbike sidecar.

25 ml (1 fl oz) Cointreau
50 ml (2 fl oz) brandy
25 ml (1 fl oz) fresh lemon juice
ice cubes
orange rind and cocktail cherry,
** to decorate**

Put the Cointreau, brandy and lemon juice into a shaker, add some ice cubes and shake vigorously. Strain into a chilled cocktail glass. Decorate with an orange rind spiral and a cocktail cherry on a cocktail stick.

Spiced Sidecar

*Morgan Spiced Rum has a mellow spicy flavour that tastes especially good when enhanced with orange and lemon in this cocktail **(left)**.*

Put the lemon juice, rum, brandy and Cointreau into a shaker with some ice cubes and shake well. Strain into an old-fashioned glass filled with ice and decorate with lemon and orange twists.

juice of ½ lemon
25 ml (1 fl oz) Morgan
** Spiced Rum**
25 ml (1 fl oz) brandy
25 ml (1 fl oz) Cointreau
ice cubes
lemon and orange rind,
** to decorate**

Sangria

The name for this bright red concoction **(left)** is derived from the Spanish word *sangre*, which means blood. Sangria is a sociable drink, so quadruple all the ingredients and drink it with friends.

37.5 ml (1½ fl oz) Spanish
  brandy
75 ml (3 fl oz) red wine
50 ml (2 fl oz) orange juice
ice cubes
soda water
lemon slices, to decorate

Pour the brandy, red wine and orange juice into a highball glass over ice. Stir, top up with soda water and decorate with lemon slices.

Gage's 'Secret' Sangria

*Gage's 'Secret' Sangria **(right)** ought to be served in a jug, preferably in the company of friends. The mix of gin, brandy and Curaçao not only makes this version more potent than the classic, it also gives it far more depth of flavour.*

Fill a highball glass with ice cubes, build the ingredients in the order given, then decorate with apple and orange wedges.

ice cubes
25 ml (1 fl oz) gin
50 ml (2 fl oz) Spanish brandy
25 ml (1 fl oz) orange Curaçao
250 ml (8 fl oz) dry red wine
250 ml (8 fl oz) lemonade
cinnamon stick, to stir
apple and orange wedges,
  to decorate

Brandy Fix

A fix is a potent sweet drink, usually served over crushed ice in an old-fashioned glass **(left)**.

crushed ice

2 teaspoons sugar syrup
  (see page 10)

32.5 ml (1¼ fl oz) fresh
  lemon juice

12.5 ml (½ fl oz) cherry brandy

25 ml (1 fl oz) brandy

lemon rind spiral, to decorate

Fill an old-fashioned glass with crushed ice. Pour all of the ingredients into the glass and decorate with a lemon rind spiral.

Bourbon Fixed

The morello cherry purée in this twist **(right)** is available in large grocery stores, or can be made by liquidizing pitted cherries with a little sugar syrup.

Put the Bourbon, cherry purée, lime juice and sugar syrup into a shaker with some ice cubes and shake to mix. Strain into an old-fashioned glass filled with ice cubes and decorate with lime rind.

50 ml (2 fl oz) Bourbon whiskey

25 ml (1 fl oz) morello
  cherry purée

1 tablespoon fresh lime juice

2 teaspoons sugar syrup
  (see page 10)

ice cubes

lime rind spirals, to decorate

the classic

Between the Sheets

An orange-flavoured drink that delivers a powerful punch **(right)**. White rum has a much lighter flavour than dark rum, complementing the flavour of the Cointreau and brandy.

12.5 ml (½ fl oz) brandy
12.5 ml (½ fl oz) white rum
12.5 ml (½ fl oz) Cointreau
25 ml (1 fl oz) orange juice
ice cubes
orange rind, to decorate

Put the brandy, rum, Cointreau and orange juice into a shaker, add some ice and shake to mix. Strain into a chilled cocktail glass and decorate with orange rind.

with a twist

From the Rafters

*Hazelnut liqueur brings a nutty note to this drink **(left),** and the cherry slices at the bottom of the glass provide an end-of-drink treat, having soaked up all the wonderful flavours.*

Put the brandy, Frangelico, Cointreau and pineapple juice into a shaker with some ice cubes and shake to mix. Strain into a chilled cocktail glass and decorate with cherry slices, which will sink to the bottom of the glass.

25 ml (1 fl oz) brandy
1 tablespoon Frangelico
 hazelnut liqueur
25 ml (1 fl oz) Cointreau
25 ml (1 fl oz) pineapple juice
ice cubes
cherry slices, to decorate

Metropolitan

The classic recipe for a Metropolitan consists of brandy, sweet vermouth, sugar and bitters **(right)**.

25 ml (1 fl oz) brandy
25 ml (1 fl oz) sweet vermouth
½ teaspoon sugar syrup
** (see page 10)**
3–4 dashes Angostura bitters
cracked ice cubes

Put the brandy, vermouth, sugar syrup and bitters into a shaker with the cracked ice cubes and shake well. Strain into a chilled cocktail glass.

Big City Dog

*A brandy balloon allows the drinker to swirl this drink **(left)** around inside, warming it against their cupped hands to release the aromas.*

Put the bitters into a brandy balloon and swirl to coat the inside. Turn the glass upside down and let it drain. Put the brandy, green Chartreuse and cherry brandy into a mixing glass with some ice cubes and stir well, then double-strain into the brandy balloon.

2 dashes Peychaud's bitters
25 ml (1 fl oz) brandy
12.5 ml (½ fl oz) green
** Chartreuse**
12.5 ml (½ fl oz) cherry brandy
ice cubes

93

Brandy Crusta

A Crusta combines a spirit with lemon juice and Angostura bitters
and is traditionally served with a spiral of orange or lemon rind **(right)**.

lemon wedge
caster sugar
50 ml (2 fl oz) brandy
12.5 ml (½ fl oz) orange
  Curaçao
12.5 ml (½ fl oz)
  Maraschino liqueur
25 ml (1 fl oz) fresh lemon juice
3 dashes Angostura bitters
ice cubes
lemon rind, to decorate

Moisten the rim of a chilled cocktail glass
with the lemon wedge, then dip it in the
caster sugar. Put the brandy, Curaçao,
Maraschino, lemon juice and bitters into a
shaker with some ice cubes and shake
well. Strain into the cocktail glass and
decorate with lemon rind.

Rum Crusta

As well as brandy, a Crusta can be made with gin, rum or whisky. This one
uses the rich flavour of dark rum with the zesty tang of Cointreau.

*Moisten the rim of an old-fashioned glass
with the lime wedge and dip it in caster
sugar. Put the rum, Cointreau, Maraschino
and lime juice into a shaker with some ice
cubes and mix well. Strain into an old-
fashioned glass filled with crushed ice and
decorate with the two grapes.*

lime wedge
caster sugar
50 ml (2 fl oz) dark rum
25 ml (1 fl oz) Cointreau
2 teaspoons Maraschino liqueur
2 teaspoons fresh lime juice
ice cubes
crushed ice
2 grapes, to decorate

Piña Colada

This must be one of the best-known cocktails **(right)**, supposedly invented in a bar in San Juan, Puerto Rico.

50 ml (2 fl oz) white rum
50 ml (2 fl oz) coconut milk
50 ml (2 fl oz) pineapple juice
crushed ice
pineapple wedges, to decorate

Put the rum, coconut milk and pineapple juice into a blender with some crushed ice and blend until slushy. Serve in a hurricane glass and decorate with pineapple wedges.

Lobsters on South Beach

*The mango purée used in this twist **(left)** is available from good grocery stores, or you can make your own by liquidizing half a skinless fresh mango.*

Put the two rums, mango purée, mandarin juice, coconut cream and pineapple chunks into a blender with some crushed ice and blend. Serve in a large highball glass and decorate with a pineapple leaf and mango slices.

25 ml (1 fl oz) white rum
25 ml (1 fl oz) Coconut rum
25 ml (1 fl oz) mango purée
50 ml (2 fl oz) mandarin juice
** (fresh if possible)**
25 ml (1 fl oz) coconut cream
4 fresh pineapple chunks
crushed ice
pineapple leaf and mango
** slices, to decorate**

the classic Cuba Libre

The first rum'n'coke is thought to have been mixed for some off-duty American soldiers at a bar in Old Havana at the turn of the 20th century, following the Spanish-American War **(right)**. The soldiers toasted the newly freed Cuba, with their former battle cry, '¡Cuba Libre!' ('Free Cuba!').

ice cubes
50 ml (2 fl oz) golden rum
juice of ½ lime
Coca-Cola, to top up
lime wedges, to decorate

Fill a highball glass with ice cubes, pour over the rum and lime juice and stir to mix. Top up with Coca-Cola and decorate with lime wedges.

with a twist *First the Money*

*An interesting twist with flavours of mint and coffee **(left)**. If you can't get Toussaint, try Kahlúa instead.*

Cut the lime into wedges and muddle in a highball glass with the crème de menthe. Fill the glass with crushed ice and add the rum and Toussaint. Top up with Coca-Cola and serve.

1 lime
**1 teaspoon white crème
 de menthe**
crushed ice
25 ml (1 fl oz) dark rum
**20 ml (³⁄₄ fl oz) Toussaint
 coffee liqueur**
Coca-Cola

Daiquiri

the classic **Daiquiri**

A refreshing white rum, lime and sugar beverage (**left**) invented in the early 20th century by Jennings S. Cox, an American working in the mines of a small Cuban town called Daiquirí.

cracked ice
juice of 2 limes
1 teaspoon sugar syrup
 (see page 10)
75 ml (3 fl oz) white rum
lime wheel, to decorate

Put lots of cracked ice into a shaker. Pour the lime juice, sugar syrup and rum over the ice. Shake thoroughly, then strain into a chilled cocktail glass and decorate with the lime wheel.

with a twist *Frozen Mango and Mint Spiced Daiquiri*

There are many variations on the Daiquiri, including frozen fruit Daiquiris and those made with mellow dark rum. This one (right) uses spiced rum, mango and mint, and is a complex yet subtle blend.

Put the lime juice, sugar syrup, rum, mango and mint leaves in a blender with some crushed ice and blend well. Pour into a large champagne saucer and decorate with a mango slice and a mint sprig.

25 ml (1 fl oz) fresh lime juice
2 teaspoons sugar syrup
 (see page 10)
50 ml (2 fl oz) Morgan
 Spiced Rum
½ ripe mango, peeled and
 roughly chopped
6 mint leaves
crushed ice
mango slice and mint sprig,
 to decorate

the classic

Mai Tai

Created in 1944 by restaurateur Victor 'Trader Vic' Bergeron and named for its accolade by the first customer to try it (Mrs Carrie Wright of Tahiti): 'Mai Tai ... Roe Aé!', which is Tahitian for 'Out of this world!' **(left)**. Orgeat is an almond-flavoured syrup.

50 ml (2 fl oz) golden rum
12.5 ml (½ fl oz) ml
 orange Curaçao
12.5 ml (½ fl oz) orgeat syrup
juice of 1 lime
ice cubes
crushed ice
2 teaspoons Woods Navy Rum
lime rind and mint sprig,
 to decorate

Put the rum, Curaçao, orgeat syrup and lime juice into a shaker with some ice cubes and shake well. Strain into an old-fashioned glass over crushed ice, float the Navy Rum on top and decorate with lime rind and a mint sprig.

with a twist

My Tie Collection

The combination of golden rum, apple juice and fresh mint is the basis for this fantastically refreshing twist – great flavours and a great drink (right)!

Put the golden rum, apple juice, lime juice, orgeat syrup and mint leaves into a shaker with some ice cubes and shake well. Strain over ice into a highball glass, float the Navy Rum on top and decorate with a cocktail cherry, pineapple wedge and lemon slice.

50 ml (2 fl oz) golden rum
25 ml (1 fl oz) apple juice
12.5 ml (½ fl oz) fresh
 lime juice
dash orgeat syrup
6 mint leaves
ice cubes
2 teaspoons Wood's Navy Rum
cocktail cherry, pineapple
 wedge and lemon slice,
 to decorate

103

the classic

Mojito

A cooling, effervescent cocktail **(left)** born – thanks to Prohibition – amid Cuba's thriving international bar culture. Probably derived from the Mint Julep (see page 130), it was popularized by the legendary bartenders of Cuba's El Floridita and La Bodeguita del Medio bars during the 1930s and '40s.

12 mint leaves or small sprigs
12.5 ml (½ fl oz) sugar syrup
 (see page 10)
1 lime, cut into 6 wedges
crushed ice
50 ml (2 fl oz) white rum
soda water

Muddle the mint with the sugar syrup and 4 of the lime wedges in a highball glass. Fill the glass with crushed ice, add the rum and stir, then top up with soda water. Decorate with the remaining lime wedges.

with a twist

Apple-soaked Mojito

*Apple and mint make a really refreshing combination, and this drink **(right)** is the perfect summer party drink.*

Muddle the mint, lime and sugar syrup in a shaker. Fill a highball glass with crushed ice. Add the rum to the shaker and shake well. Do not add ice to the shaker. Strain the drink into the highball glass and top up with apple juice. Decorate with a mint sprig and apple slices.

8 mint leaves
½ lime, cut into wedges
2 teaspoons sugar syrup
 (see page 10)
crushed ice
50 ml (2 fl oz) golden rum
 (e.g. Havana 3-year-old)
25 ml (1 fl oz) apple juice
mint sprig and red apple slices,
 to decorate

Zombie

the classic

A potent draught **(right)** probably invented by Don Beach of Hollywood's Don the Beachcomber restaurant, to revive the spirits of a regular who often described himself as feeling like the living dead!

25 ml (1 fl oz) dark rum
25 ml (1 fl oz) white rum
12.5 ml (½ fl oz) golden rum
12.5 ml (½ fl oz) apricot brandy
juice of ½ lime
1 teaspoon grenadine
50 ml (2 fl oz) pineapple juice
12.5 ml (½ fl oz) sugar syrup
  (see page 10)
ice cubes
2 teaspoons overproof rum
pineapple wedge and leaf and
  pinch of sugar, to decorate

Put the three rums, apricot brandy, lime juice, grenadine, pineapple juice and sugar syrup into a shaker with some ice cubes and shake well. Pour into a chilled glass without straining, and float the overproof rum on top. Decorate with a pineapple wedge and leaf, and sprinkle a pinch of sugar over the top.

Kinky Witch

with a twist

Crème de mure, adds a powerfully sweet zing to this great sour twist **(left)**.

Put the two rums, Curaçao, crème de mure, orgeat syrup, orange juice and grapefruit juice into a shaker with some ice cubes and shake well. Strain into a highball glass filled with ice cubes, float the overproof rum over the surface and decorate with the grapefruit wedges.

25 ml (1 fl oz) Havana Club
  3-year-old rum
25 ml (1 fl oz) Havana Club
  Silver Dry rum
12.5 ml (½ fl oz) orange Curaçao
12.5 ml (½ fl oz) crème de mure
12.5 ml (½ fl oz) orgeat syrup
50 ml (2 fl oz) orange juice
50 ml (2 fl oz) grapefruit juice
ice cubes
2 teaspoons overproof rum
grapefruit wedges, to decorate

Egg Nog

A traditional wintertime drink served dusted with grated nutmeg, an egg nog **(right)** contains brandy, rum or Bourbon or a combination of these three, plus an egg, sugar and milk or cream.

25 ml (1 fl oz) brandy
25 ml (1 fl oz) dark rum
1 egg
1 teaspoon sugar syrup (see page 10)
75 ml (3 fl oz) full cream milk
grated nutmeg, to decorate

Put the brandy, rum, egg and sugar syrup into a shaker and shake well, then strain into a large goblet. Add the milk then sprinkle some grated nutmeg on top to decorate.

Banana Custard

A comforting concoction (left) based on a popular childhood dessert – just don't let the kids near it!

Put the brandy, rum, banana liqueur, egg, single cream and mashed banana into a shaker with the ice cubes and shake well. Strain into a goblet and decorate with the banana slices.

25 ml (1 fl oz) brandy
25 ml (1 fl oz) golden rum
12.5 ml (½ fl oz) banana liqueur
1 egg
25 ml (1 fl oz) single cream
½ ripe banana, mashed
ice cubes
3 banana slices, to decorate

Planter's Punch

A 19th-century drink **(right)** enjoyed by generations of sugar planters in Jamaica. There are plenty of recipe variations but all call for well-aged Jamaica rum for authenticity.

50 ml (2 fl oz) well-aged Jamaica rum (such as Appleton V/X)
50 ml (2 fl oz) orange juice
1 tablespoon fresh lime juice
2 dashes Angostura bitters
1 teaspoon caster sugar
ice cubes
lemon wedges, to decorate

Put the rum, orange and lime juices, bitters and sugar into a shaker with some ice cubes. Shake until a frost forms on the outside of the shaker then strain into a large old-fashioned glass filled with ice cubes. Decorate with the orange slices.

Chetta's Punch

Named after a Kentish legend renowned for his alcohol consumption, this short, sturdy drink (left) makes the perfect pick-me-up.

Put the rum, blackcurrant cordial, lemon juice and bitters in a mixing glass with some ice cubes and stir well. Strain into an old-fashioned glass filled with ice cubes and decorate with orange slices.

50 ml (2 fl oz) Lamb's Navy Rum
25 ml (1 fl oz) undiluted blackcurrant cordial
1 tablespoon fresh lemon juice
6 dashes orange bitters
ice cubes
orange slices, to decorate

111

the classic **Bacardi Cocktail**

After the Bacardi Company tired of seeing its name used as a generic term for a rum cocktail, in 1936 a New York State Supreme court ruled that it is illegal to make this cocktail without Bacardi rum **(left)**.

50 ml (2 fl oz) Bacardi white rum
20 ml (¾ fl oz) fresh lime juice
12.5 ml (½ fl oz) grenadine
ice cubes
lime rind, to decorate

Put the rum, lime juice and grenadine into a shaker with some ice cubes and shake vigorously. Strain into a chilled cocktail glass and decorate with lime rind.

with a twist *Bacardi Cocktail II*

The Chambord in this cocktail (right) adds honey and raspberry notes, and the aged rum has a more mellow flavour than the white rum used in the classic.

Put the rum, apple juice, Chambord and sugar syrup in a mixing glass with some ice cubes and stir until chilled. Strain into a chilled cocktail glass and decorate with cocktail cherries.

37.5 ml (1½ fl oz) Bacardi 8-year-old rum
25 ml (1 fl oz) apple juice
2 teaspoons Chambord liqueur
1 teaspoon sugar syrup (see page 10)
ice cubes
2 cocktail cherries, to decorate

113

Whisky Daisy

Daisies are refreshing, spirit-based drinks, dating from the 19th century, that include grenadine or a sweet liqueur and lemon or lime juice. The Whisky Daisy **(right)** is probably the best known.

50 ml (2 fl oz) Scotch whisky or Bourbon whiskey
25 ml (1 fl oz) fresh lemon juice
1 teaspoon caster sugar
1 teaspoon grenadine
ice cubes
soda water, to top up (optional)
lemon rind, to decorate

Put the whisky, lemon juice, caster sugar and grenadine in a shaker with some ice cubes and shake well. Strain into an old-fashioned glass filled with ice cubes and top up with soda, if you like. Decorate with lemon rind.

Vanilla Daisy

Vanilla syrup and grenadine add a smooth, sweet note to this Bourbon-based daisy (left).

Put the Bourbon, lemon juice and vanilla syrup in a shaker with some crushed ice and shake well. Strain into an old-fashioned glass filled with crushed ice then drizzle the grenadine through the drink. Decorate with cocktail cherries.

50 ml (2 fl oz) Bourbon whiskey
25 ml (1 fl oz) fresh lemon juice
25 ml (1 fl oz) vanilla syrup
crushed ice
1 teaspoon grenadine
2 cocktail cherries, to decorate

115

Manhattan

A very old cocktail (right) supposedly created at New York's Manhattan Club at the request of Sir Winston Churchill's mother, Lady Randolph Churchill, who was hosting a party for a politician. Originally made with rye whiskey, today it is more commonly made with Bourbon.

50 ml (2 fl oz) rye or
 Bourbon whiskey
25 ml (1 fl oz) extra
 dry vermouth
4 dashes Angostura bitters
ice cubes
cocktail cherry, to decorate

Put the whiskey, vermouth and bitters into a mixing glass with some ice cubes and stir. Strain into a chilled cocktail glass. Decorate with a cocktail cherry.

St Clements' Manhattan

Orange- and lemon-infused Bourbon add a citrus tang to this Manhattan (left), giving it a lighter, fruitier flavour than the classic version.

Put the two whiskeys, vermouth and bitters into a mixing glass with some ice and stir well. Strain into a chilled cocktail glass and decorate with orange and lemon twists.

25 ml (1 fl oz) orange-infused
 Bourbon whiskey
25 ml (1 fl oz) lemon-infused
 Bourbon whiskey
1 tablespoon sweet vermouth
4 dashes of Angostura bitters
ice cubes
orange and lemon twists,
 to decorate

Whisky Mac

A warming slug **(right)** made with equal measures of Scotch and ginger wine, this is a delicious winter pick-me-up.

3–4 ice cubes
25 ml (1 fl oz) Scotch whisky
25 ml (1 fl oz) ginger wine

Put the ice cubes in an old-fashioned glass. Pour the whisky and ginger wine over the ice and stir lightly.

Early Night

Ginger wine is made from grapes and flavoured with ginger and other spices. It complements the lemon, honey and whisky flavours of this warm drink (left) exceptionally well.

Put the lemon juice and honey in a toddy glass and stir well. Add the Scotch and continue stirring. Stir in the boiling water then add the ginger wine immediately. Stir continuously whilst drinking. Decorate with a lemon wheel.

1 tablespoon fresh lemon juice
25 ml (1 fl oz) clear honey
25 ml (1 fl oz) J&B Scotch
  whisky
50 ml (2 fl oz) boiling water
25 ml (1 fl oz) ginger wine
lemon wheel, to decorate

119

Algonquin

A blend of sweet and sour, combining pineapple juice and vermouth with rye **(right)**. Rye whiskey is made almost entirely from rye grain, whereas Bourbon is made from three grains.

25 ml (1 fl oz) pineapple juice
25 ml (1 fl oz) dry vermouth
50 ml (2 fl oz) rye whiskey
ice cubes

Pour the pineapple juice, vermouth and whiskey into a shaker, add some ice cubes and shake well. Strain into a chilled martini glass.

with a twist # *Harlequin*

Canadian Club whisky is aged in white oak, giving it a lighter, smoother taste than most scotches and bourbons. It works particularly well with sweet vermouth in this cocktail (left).

Muddle the grapes, vermouth and bitters in an old-fashioned glass. Half fill the glass with crushed ice and stir well. Add the whisky and top with crushed ice. Decorate with 2 grapes.

5 white grapes
12.5 ml ($^{1}/_{2}$ fl oz) sweet
 vermouth
6 dashes of orange bitters
crushed ice
50 ml (2 fl oz) Canadian
 Club whisky
2 grapes, to decorate

Lynchburg Lemonade

A classic based on Jack Daniel's 'sour mash' Tennessee whiskey, and created for the Jack Daniel's distillery in Lynchburg, Tennessee.

37.5 ml (1½ fl oz) Jack Daniel's Tennessee whiskey
25 ml (1 fl oz) Cointreau
25 ml (1 fl oz) fresh lemon juice
ice cubes
lemonade, to top up
lemon slices, to decorate

Put the whiskey, Cointreau and lemon juice into a shaker with some ice cubes and shake well, then strain into a highball glass filled with ice cubes. Top up with lemonade and stir. Decorate with lemon slices.

with a twist

A Kiwi in Tennessee

This twist (left) maintains the sourness of the classic, and uses kiwi to impart an intense fruity flavour. A refreshing drink for whiskey lovers.

Muddle the kiwi in a cocktail shaker, then add the whiskey, kiwi schnapps and lemon juice. Add some ice cubes and shake well then strain into a highball glass filled with ice cubes. Stir and top up with lemonade. Decorate with kiwi slices.

½ skinless kiwi fruit
50 ml (2 fl oz) Jack Daniel's Tennessee whiskey
25 ml (1 fl oz) kiwi schnapps
25 ml (1 fl oz) fresh lemon juice
ice cubes
lemonade, to top up
kiwi slices, to decorate

Old Fashioned

Short for 'old-fashioned whiskey cocktail', and with a glass named after it, this is another classic **(left)** whose authentic recipe is hotly debated. One theory is that it was invented at the Pendennis Club in Louisville, Kentucky, in the late 1880s for retired Confederate officer and Bourbon proprietor, James E. Pepper.

50 ml (2 fl oz) Bourbon whiskey
ice cubes
1 teaspoon sugar syrup
  (see page 10)
4 dashes Angostura bitters
orange twist, to decorate

Put the whiskey in an old-fashioned glass and add a few ice cubes. Continue building the ingredients with the ice, then decorate with the orange twist.

Rum Refashioned

*This twist **(right)** uses rum instead of Bourbon whiskey. Try to find a good brand of aged rum, such as Havana 7-year-old.*

Put the sugar cube into an old-fashioned glass then splash in the bitters, add 2 ice cubes and stir. Add a quarter of the rum and another 2 ice cubes and stir. Continue building, and stirring, with the rum and ice cubes, adding sugar syrup to taste. Decorate with the lime twist.

1 brown sugar cube
4 dashes Angostura bitters
ice cubes
50 ml (2 fl oz) aged rum
dash sugar syrup (see page 10)
lime twist, to decorate

Rusty Nail

An after-dinner drink **(right)** whose name is probably due to its colour rather than the tale of immigrant Scottish bartenders stirring the cocktail with a rusty nail before serving it to their American patrons.

ice cubes
37.5 ml (1½ fl oz) Scotch whisky
25 ml (1 fl oz) Drambuie

Fill an old-fashioned glass with ice cubes and pour the Scotch whisky and Drambuie over them.

with a twist

Silky Pin

*The Drambuie Cream Liqueur used in this twist **(left)** is the creamy version of Drambuie, a Scottish liqueur flavoured with herbs and heather honey.*

Fill an old-fashioned glass with ice cubes and pour in the Scotch whisky and Drambuie Cream Liqueur.

ice cubes
25 ml (1 fl oz) Scotch whisky
25 ml (1 fl oz) Drambuie
  Cream Liqueur

Rhett Butler

A dry concoction combining Bourbon whiskey and cranberry juice with a hint of lime **(left)**.

50 ml (2 fl oz) Bourbon whiskey
100 ml (4 fl oz) cranberry juice
2 tablespoons sugar syrup
  (see page 10)
1 tablespoon fresh lime juice
ice cubes
lime slices, to decorate

Put the Bourbon, cranberry juice, sugar syrup and lime juice into a shaker with some ice cubes and mix well. Fill an old-fashioned glass with ice cubes and strain the cocktail into it. Decorate with lime slices.

Big Buff

*A fruity version of the Rhett Butler, containing a mixture of berries **(right)**. Buffalo Trace Bourbon has a delicious vanilla character.*

Muddle the berries and Chambord in a cocktail shaker. Add the lime juice, Bourbon, cranberry juice and some ice cubes. Shake, then pour without straining into the highball glass, and decorate with blueberries.

1 strawberry
3 raspberries
3 blueberries
2 teaspoons Chambord liqueur
ice cubes
dash of fresh lime juice
50 ml (2 fl oz) Buffalo Trace
  Bourbon whiskey
75 ml (3 fl oz) cranberry juice
additional blueberries,
  to decorate

129

the classic Mint Julep

The earliest written reference dates this aperitif – the ultimate Deep South cocktail – to 1803 **(left)**.

10 fresh mint leaves
1 teaspoon sugar syrup
 (see page 10)
4 dashes Angostura Bitters
crushed ice
50 ml (2 fl oz) Bourbon whiskey
mint sprig, to decorate

Muddle the mint, sugar syrup and bitters in a highball glass. Fill the glass with crushed ice then add the Bourbon. Stir well and decorate with a mint sprig.

with a twist *The Vatican Julep*

A very minty julep – the drink (right) contains crème de menthe and the mint leaves are blended into the drink to bring out a more intense flavour.

Fill a highball glass with crushed ice. Put the whiskey, crème de menthe, lime juice, sugar syrup, mint and bitters in a blender and mix well. Pour the mixture over the ice and top up with more crushed ice. Decorate with a mint sprig.

crushed ice
50 ml (2 fl oz) Bourbon whiskey
2 teaspoons crème de menthe
12.5 ml (½ fl oz) fresh lime juice
12.5 ml (½ fl oz) sugar syrup
 (see page 10)
6 mint leaves
4 dashes Angostura bitters
mint sprig, to decorate

Godfather

Popular variations on this old classic (left) replace the Scotch with vodka to make a Godmother, and with brandy to make a Godchild.

50 ml (2 fl oz) J&B Rare Scotch whisky
25 ml (1 fl oz) Amaretto di Saronno liqueur
ice cubes

Put the whisky and Amaretto into a shaker with some ice cubes and mix well. Strain into a small old-fashioned glass filled with ice cubes.

Godfather Sour

This twist (right) is a pleasing cross between a Godfather and a Whiskey Sour (see page 136). All the flavours are distinct but none is overpowering.

Put the whiskey, Amaretto, lemon juice and sugar syrup into a shaker with some ice cubes and mix well. Strain into a small old-fashioned glass filled with ice cubes and decorate with lemon slices.

37.5 ml (1½ fl oz) Bourbon whiskey
25 ml (1 fl oz) Amaretto di Saronno liqueur
25 ml (1 fl oz) lemon juice
1 teaspoon sugar syrup (see page 10)
ice cubes
lemon slices, to decorate

the classic | Irish Coffee

A blend of strong coffee, Irish whiskey and a little sugar, served in a wine glass and topped by a float of double cream **(left)**. There are lots of variations using virtually any liqueur in place of the whiskey.

25 ml (1 fl oz) Irish whiskey
hot filter coffee
lightly whipped cream
sprinkle of ground coffee,
** to decorate**

Place a bar spoon in a large wine glass, add the whiskey, then top up with coffee and stir. Heat the cream very slightly and pour into the bowl of the spoon on top of the coffee to get a good float. Decorate with a pinch of ground coffee.

with a twist | *Mexican Marshmallow Mocha*

*An indulgent chocolatey version **(right)** with melted marshmallows and whipped cream on top. This makes a great follow-up to dessert at a dinner party.*

Put the cocoa powder in a toddy glass, add the Kahlúa and coffee and stir until mixed. Drop in the mini marshmallows and float the cream on top. Decorate with cocoa powder.

2 teaspoons cocoa powder
25 ml (1 fl oz) Kahlúa
** coffee liqueur**
100 ml (3½ fl oz) hot
** filter coffee**
mini marshmallows
whipped cream
cocoa powder, to decorate

Whiskey Sour

An inspired blend of sour and sweet, this is probably the best-known and best-loved sour **(left)**. The egg white thickens the drink and smoothes it, giving it a foamy head and heavy texture.

50 ml (2 fl oz) Bourbon whiskey
37.5 ml (1½ fl oz) fresh lemon juice
1 egg white
2 tablespoons sugar syrup (see page 10)
4 dashes Angostura bitters
ice cubes
cocktail cherry and lemon slice, to decorate

Put the whiskey, lemon juice, egg white, sugar syrup and bitters into a shaker with some ice cubes and mix well. Strain into a sour glass filled with ice cubes and decorate with a cocktail cherry and lemon slice on a cocktail stick.

Flower Power Sour

A totally different sour (right) made with vodka and flavoured with mandarin and elderflower – fresh and fragrant.

Put the vodka, Mandarine Napoléon, elderflower cordial, sugar syrup and lemon juice into a shaker with some ice cubes. Shake, then strain into an old-fashioned glass filled with ice cubes and decorate with orange rind.

37.5 ml (1½ fl oz) Absolut Mandrin vodka
12.5 ml (½ fl oz) Mandarine Napoléon liqueur
2 teaspoons elderflower cordial
2 teaspoons sugar syrup (see page 10)
25 ml (1 fl oz) fresh lemon juice
ice cubes
orange rind, to decorate

Bellini

A refreshing drink made with Champagne and peach juice or purée **(right)**, which originated in Harry's Bar in Venice.

50 ml (2 fl oz) peach juice
100 ml (4 fl oz) chilled
Champagne
dash of grenadine (optional)
peach slice, to decorate

Mix the peach juice and chilled Champagne in a large champagne flute with a dash of grenadine, if using. Decorate with a peach slice.

Mango Bellini

*Peach and mango purée for this cocktail **(left)** can easily be made by liquidizing the skinless flesh of either fruit.*

Put the ice cubes, peach purée, mango purée and mango liqueur in a cocktail shaker and shake. Strain the contents into a large martini glass, then pour in the Champagne very slowly. Decorate with a mango slice and twist.

ice cubes
12.5 ml ($\frac{1}{2}$ fl oz) peach purée
12.5 ml ($\frac{1}{2}$ fl oz) mango purée
25 ml (1 fl oz) Santory
mango liqueur
100 ml (4 fl oz) chilled
Champagne
mango slice and twist,
to decorate

139

Classic Champagne Cocktail

This cocktail **(left)** was certainly around in the 1930s and may even date back to the 19th century.

1 sugar cube
1–2 dashes Angostura bitters
25 ml (1 fl oz) brandy
100 ml (4 fl oz) chilled Champagne
orange twist, to decorate

Put the sugar cube into a chilled cocktail or Champagne glass and saturate with the bitters. Add the brandy, then fill the glass with the chilled Champagne. Decorate with the orange twist.

The Classic's Classic

By using Grand Marnier instead of brandy, this version (right) has a delicious orange flavour.

Saturate the sugar cube with the bitters then drop it into a Champagne flute. Add the Grand Marnier then top up with the chilled Champagne. Place the orange rind in the drink to decorate.

1 sugar cube
2 dashes of Angostura bitters
25 ml (1 fl oz) Grand Marnier
100 ml (4 fl oz) chilled Champagne
orange rind, to decorate

Kir Royale

White wine flavoured with crème de cassis (a French blackcurrant-flavoured liqueur) and served as an aperitif is called Kir. Use Champagne instead of wine and you have a Kir Royale **(right)**!

2 teaspoons crème de cassis
chilled Champagne, to top up

Pour the crème de cassis into a chilled Champagne flute and top up with some chilled Champagne.

with a twist

Kitsch Revolt

*The strawberry purée for this twist **(left)** can be bought from good grocery stores, or made by liquidizing hulled ripe strawberries.*

Put the vodka, strawberry purée and some ice cubes into a shaker and shake briefly. Strain into a martini glass then top up with chilled Champagne and stir.

25 ml (1 fl oz) Absolut
   Kurant vodka
12.5 ml (½ fl oz)
   strawberry purée
ice cubes
100 ml (4 fl oz) chilled
   Champagne

the classic — Grand Mimosa

This is a Buck's Fizz (see page 148) with a difference! It was created in 1925 at the Ritz Hotel in Paris and named after the mimosa plant – probably because of its trembling leaves, which are rather like the gentle fizz of this mixture **(left)**.

25 ml (1 fl oz) Grand Marnier
50 ml (2 fl oz) orange juice,
chilled
chilled Champagne

Pour the Grand Marnier and orange juice into a Champagne flute and top up with chilled Champagne.

with a twist — Grandaddy Mimosa

A sparkling twist (right) using golden rum instead of Grand Marnier, with a splash of lemon juice to impart a fresh, zesty flavour.

Put the rum, orange juice and lemon juice into a shaker with some ice cubes and shake to mix. Strain into a large Champagne flute then top up with chilled Champagne. Decorate with an orange twist, and drop in the grenadine.

25 ml (1 fl oz) Havana Club
3-year-old rum
25 ml (1 fl oz) orange juice
12.5 ml (½ fl oz) fresh
lemon juice
ice cubes
chilled Champagne, to top up
orange twist, to decorate
dash of grenadine

145

Ritz Fizz

The Ritz Fizz **(right)** was originally created at the Ritz Hotel in London in about 1930.

25 ml (1 fl oz) blue Curaçao
25 ml (1 fl oz) fresh lemon juice
25 ml (1 fl oz) Amaretto
 di Saronno
chilled Champagne, to top up
lemon rind, to decorate

Pour the Curaçao, lemon juice and Amaretto into a champagne flute and top up with chilled Champagne. Stir gently to mix and decorate with the lemon rind.

Ritz Fizz II

*The blend of pear and blackcurrant liqueurs as the base of this delicious champagne cocktail **(left)** make it a little too easy to drink!*

Put the crème de cassis and Poire William in a mixing glass with some ice cubes and stir to mix well. Strain into a Champagne flute and top up with Champagne. Decorate with skinless pear slices.

12.5 ml (½ fl oz) crème
 de cassis
12.5 ml (½ fl oz) Poire William
ice cubes
chilled Champagne, to top up
skinless pear slices,
 to decorate

the classic

Buck's Fizz

Chilled orange juice and Champagne make up this celebratory drink **(right)**. If you're making large quantities for a party in a jug, don't forget to leave room for the Champagne to fizz up.

50 ml (2 fl oz) chilled orange juice
150 ml (6 fl oz) chilled Champagne

Pour the chilled orange juice into a cocktail glass and add the chilled Champagne.

with a twist

Buck's Twizz

*Maraschino is a liqueur from Italy, flavoured with sour maraschino cherries and their crushed stones, and adds wonderful flavour to this drink **(left)**.*

Pour the orange juice and Maraschino into a chilled Champagne saucer, then add the vodka and Champagne at the same time (this prevents excessive fizzing). Decorate with a rindless pink grapefruit wheel.

25 ml (1 fl oz) chilled orange juice
12.5 ml (½ fl oz) Maraschino liqueur
25 ml (1 fl oz) Absolut Mandrin vodka
chilled Champagne, to top up
rindless pink grapefruit wheel, to decorate

Russian Spring Punch

This beautifully coloured cocktail **(left)** is an excellent, festive drink to celebrate any occasion.

ice cubes
1.25 ml (½ fl oz) cremé de
  cassis
25 ml (1 fl oz) fresh lemon juice
2 tablespoons sugar syrup
  (see page 10)
chilled Champagne, to top up
50 ml (2 fl oz) Absolut vodka
lemon slice and berries,
  to decorate

Pour the crème de cassis, lemon juice and sugar syrup into an sling glass filled with ice cubes, then pour in the Champagne and vodka together and stir. Adding the vodka at the same time as the Champagne will stop it fizzing up. Decorate with a lemon slice and berries and serve.

Parisian Spring Punch

*An all-French twist **(right)** using Calvados, an apple-flavoured liqueur from Normandy, and Noilly Prat vermouth.*

Put the Calvados, lemon juice, vermouth and caster sugar in a shaker with some ice cubes and shake to mix. Strain into a sling glass over crushed ice and top up with Champagne. Decorate with apple slices.

37.5 ml (1½ fl oz) Calvados
12.5 ml (½ fl oz) fresh
  lemon juice
12.5 ml (½ fl oz) Noilly
  Prat vermouth
1 teaspoon fine caster sugar
ice cubes
crushed ice
chilled Champagne, to top up
apple slices, to decorate

the classic

Long Island Iced Tea

A very potent brew **(left)**, supposedly created by Robert 'Rosebud' Butt of the Oak Beach Inn, Hampton Bay.

12.5 ml (½ fl oz) vodka
12.5 ml (½ fl oz) gin
12.5 ml (½ fl oz) white rum
12.5 ml (½ fl oz) tequila
12.5 ml (½ fl oz) Cointreau
12.5 ml (½ fl oz) fresh
  lemon juice
ice cubes
Coca-Cola, to top up
lemon slices, to decorate

Put the vodka, gin, rum, tequila, Cointreau and lemon juice in a cocktail shaker with some ice cubes and shake to mix. Strain into a highball glass filled with ice cubes, top up with Coca-Cola and decorate with lemon slices.

with a twist

Camber Sands Iced Tea

*The British equivalent **(right)**, actually made with tea. It is flavoured with lemon, cranberry and mint, for a deliciously refreshing drink.*

Put the vodka, iced tea, cranberry juice, mint leaves, sugar syrup and lemon juice in a shaker with some ice cubes and shake to mix. Strain into a highball glass filled with ice cubes and decorate with mint leaves and a lemon slice.

50 ml (2 fl oz) Absolut
  Citron vodka
100 ml (4 fl oz) mixed iced tea
  (made with a mixture of Earl
  Grey, English Breakfast and
  Lemon tea)
25 ml (1 fl oz) cranberry juice
6 mint leaves
dash of sugar syrup
  (see page 10)
dash of fresh lemon juice
ice cubes
lemon slice and mint leaves,
  to decorate

Caipirinha

This is the most famous Brazilian cocktail **(right)**, inspired by the Cuban Daiquiri. It is made with cachaça, a fiery clear Brazilian spirit distilled from sugar cane.

6 lime wedges
2 teaspoons brown sugar
crushed ice
50 ml (2 fl oz) cachaça

Put all the lime wedges in an old-fashioned glass and add the brown sugar. Muddle well, mashing the limes and sugar together. Top with the crushed ice and add the cachaça. Stir well and serve with a stirrer.

Kiwi Caipiroska

A Caipirinha can only be made with cachaça – if it is made with vodka it is called a Caipiroska. Without a fruit flavour it can be a fairly bland drink, but with the addition of kiwi this twist is delicious (left).

Muddle the kiwi fruit, lime and sugar syrup in an old-fashioned glass. Fill the glass with crushed ice, add the vodka and stir. Add more ice then drizzle the schnapps over the surface and decorate with a kiwi wheel.

½ kiwi fruit, peeled
½ lime
2 teaspoons sugar syrup
  (see page 10)
crushed ice
50 ml (2 fl oz) vodka
2 teaspoons kiwi schnapps
kiwi wheel, to decorate

the classic # Japanese Slipper

Midori gives this cocktail **(right)** its distinctive flavour. It is a vibrant green Japanese honeydew melon-flavoured liqueur.

32.5 ml (1¼ fl oz) tequila
20 ml (¾ fl oz) Midori melon liqueur
32.5 ml (1¼ fl oz) fresh lime juice
4–5 ice cubes
lime wheel, to decorate

Pour the tequila, midori and lime juice into a shaker and add the ice cubes. Shake vigorously for about 10 seconds then strain into the cocktail glass and decorate with a lime wheel.

with a twist # *The Bed Taker*

So easy to drink yet deceptively potent, this frozen cocktail (left) cries out to be drunk in the heat of the day on a tropical beach.

Put the Midori, vodka, orange juice, melon and some crushed ice into a blender and blend until slushy. Pour into a large brandy balloon and decorate with melon slices.

25 ml (1 fl oz) Midori liqueur
25 ml (1 fl oz) vodka
25 ml (1 fl oz) orange juice
3 chunks ripe galia melon
crushed ice
melon slices, to decorate

Batida

Another Brazilian classic using cachaça, this traditional working man's drink (right) has not transferred as quickly from its native Brazil as the Caipirinha (see page 154).

50 ml (2 fl oz) cachaça
12.5 ml (½ fl oz) sugar syrup
 (see page 10)
12.5 ml (½ fl oz) fresh
 lemon juice
75 ml (3 fl oz) fruit juice of your
 choice (such as strawberry,
 pineapple or mango)
crushed ice

Fill a highball glass with crushed ice. Pour the cachaça, sugar syrup, lemon juice and fruit juice into the glass and stir to mix thoroughly before serving.

Cardamom and Raspberry Batida

Cardamom adds a fragrant spiciness to this wonderful balance of sweet and sour flavours (left).

Muddle the raspberries and raspberry purée in a mixing glass. Add the cachaça, sugar syrup, lemon juice, cardamom seeds and ice cubes and shake. Strain into a highball glass over crushed ice and decorate with lemon slices.

4 raspberries
25 ml (1 fl oz)
 puréed raspberries
50 ml (2 fl oz) cachaça
12.5 ml (½ fl oz) sugar syrup
 (see page 10)
12.5 ml (½ fl oz) lemon juice
seeds from 4 cardamom pods
ice cubes
crushed ice
lemon slices, to decorate

Grasshopper

A minty cocktail **(left)** containing equal measures of two French favourites, crème de cacao and crème de menthe.

25 ml (1 fl oz) crème de cacao
25 ml (1 fl oz) crème de menthe
mint sprig, to decorate

Float the two liqueurs into a martini glass (see page 12) and decorate with a mint sprig.

with a twist **Deaf Knees**

*The layers of chocolate, mint and orange deliver a powerful kick and an explosion of flavours as you knock back this shot **(right)**.*

Using a bar spoon, carefully layer the chocolate schnapps, crème de menthe and Grand Marnier in a shot glass, then down it in one gulp!

12.5 ml (¹/₂ fl oz) chocolate schnapps
12.5 ml (¹/₂ fl oz) crème de menthe
12.5 ml (¹/₂ fl oz) Grand Marnier

Classic Pimm's

This long summery drink is reminiscent of sophisticated garden parties and evening balls **(left)**.

50 ml (2 fl oz) Pimm's No 1
6–8 ice cubes
orange, lemon and cucumber
  slices
100 ml (4 fl oz) lemonade
mint or borage sprigs,
  to decorate

Pour the Pimm's into a highball glass and add 6–8 ice cubes and the fruit and cucumber slices, then pour in the lemonade. Serve decorated with mint or borage sprigs.

On the Lawn

More alcoholic than the original, with the addition of gin, but refreshing just the same. Ginger ale adds a delicious spiciness to the drink **(right)**.

Fill a highball glass with ice cubes then add the Pimm's No 1, gin, lemonade and ginger ale. Decorate with cucumber strips, blueberries and orange slices.

ice cubes
25 ml (1 fl oz) Pimm's No 1
25 ml (1 fl oz) gin
50 ml (2 fl oz) lemonade
50 ml (2 fl oz) ginger ale
cucumber strips, blueberries
  and orange slices, to decorate

the classic **Toblerone**

A much-loved rich creamy classic **(right)**, with all the flavours of the popular Swiss chocolate in a frozen cocktail.

1 teaspoon clear honey

25 ml (1 fl oz) Frangelico
  hazelnut liqueur

25 ml (1 fl oz) Bailey's
  Irish Cream

25 ml (1 fl oz) single cream

25 ml (1 fl oz) dark crème
  de cacao

crushed ice

chocolate shavings, to decorate

Put the honey, Frangelico, Bailey's, cream and crème de cacao in a blender with some crushed ice and blend until slushy. Pour into a hurricane glass and decorate with chocolate shavings.

with a twist *X-rated Milkshake*

*Don't be deceived by its milkshake qualities – there is a generous amount of alcohol in this twist **(left)**!*

Put the Frangelico, Bailey's, cream, crème de cacao, honey, strawberries and banana into a blender with some crushed ice and blend until slushy. Decorate the inside of a large hurricane glass with chocolate sauce and pour in the drink.

25 ml (1 fl oz) Frangelico
  hazelnut liqueur

25 ml (1 fl oz) Bailey's
  Irish Cream

25 ml (1 fl oz) single cream

25 ml (1 fl oz) dark crème
  de cacao

12.5 ml ($^1/_2$ fl oz) clear honey

4 strawberries

$^1/_3$ banana

crushed ice

25 ml (1 fl oz) chocolate sauce,
  to decorate

B-52

This short, three-layered drink **(left)** is served in a shot glass and designed to be downed in one.

12.5 ml (½ fl oz) Kahlúa coffee liqueur
12.5 ml (½ fl oz) Bailey's Irish Cream
12.5 ml (½ fl oz) Grand Marnier

Pour the Kahlúa into a shot glass. Using the back of a spoon, slowly float the Bailey's over the Kahlúa. Pour the Grand Marnier over the Bailey's in the same way. This will result in a three-layered shooter.

B-4-12

*Layered cocktails like this **(right)** will keep for at least an hour in the refrigerator, so you can make several in advance of your guests arriving.*

Pour the Amaretto into a shot glass. Using the back of a spoon, slowly float the Bailey's over the Amaretto. Pour the Absolut Kurant over the Bailey's in the same way.

12.5 ml (¹/₂ fl oz) Amaretto di Saronno
12.5 ml (¹/₂ fl oz) Bailey's Irish Cream
12.5 ml (¹/₂ fl oz) chilled Absolut Kurant vodka

Kamikaze Shooter

A classic shot featuring vodka, Cointreau and lime juice designed to be downed in one gulp **(left)**.

20 ml (¾ fl oz) Absolut vodka
20 ml (¾ fl oz) Cointreau
12.5 ml (½ fl oz) fresh lime juice
ice cubes

Put the vodka, Cointreau and lime juice into a shaker with some ice cubes, shake briefly then strain into a shot glass.

Autumn Dawn

An attractive-looking shot (right) with a hint of raspberry and honey flavour from the Chambord.

Put the vodka, Cointreau and lemon juice into a shaker with some ice cubes and shake briefly. Strain into a shot glass and carefully drop in the Chambord.

12.5 ml (¹/₂ fl oz) vodka
12.5 ml (¹/₂ fl oz) Cointreau
1 teaspoon fresh lemon juice
ice cubes
1 teaspoon Chambord liqueur

Cowboy

A layer of Bailey's on top of butterscotch schnapps, a liqueur with the delectable flavour of butter and brown sugar **(right)**.

25 ml (1 fl oz) chilled butterscotch schnapps
12.5 ml (½ fl oz) Bailey's Irish Cream

Pour the schnapps into a shot glass, then float the Bailey's on top by pouring it over the back of a spoon in contact with the liquid surface.

Cowgirl

The flavour of peach schnapps with Bailey's is a winning combination, and the slice of ripe peach adds a touch of decadence to this shot (left).

Pour the chilled schnapps into a shot glass, then layer the Bailey's on top. Place a peach wedge on the rim of the glass, to be eaten after the shot has been drunk.

25 ml (1 fl oz) chilled peach schnapps
12.5 ml (½ fl oz) Bailey's Irish Cream
peach wedge

171

Tequila Shot

The traditional way to drink tequila is to use a tall shot glass with a narrow base and a wider mouth **(right)**. Called a *caballito* (little horse), the glass is said to be modelled on the original bull's horn, from which tequila was drunk.

pinch of salt
25 ml (1 fl oz) Gold Tequila
lemon slice

Lick the salt, drink the shot, bite the lemon.

Dash-love

*A jewel of a drink **(left)** with a few drops of raspberry purée between the layers of chocolate liqueur and tequila.*

Pour the crème de cacao into a shot glass, then layer the chilled tequila over a spoon. Carefully add the raspberry purée to the surface of the liquid – it should sink and then float midway.

2 teaspoons light crème de cacao
20 ml (³⁄₄ fl oz) chilled tequila
2–3 drops raspberry purée

Vodka Shot

A very short strong drink to be consumed in a single gulp – for the unimaginative amongst us **(left)**.

25 ml (1 fl oz) chilled vodka

Pour the vodka into a shot glass, then drink it in a single gulp.

383

*The raspberry flavoured vodka with just a hint of hazelnut makes a delicious shot **(right)**, perfectly finished with a sugar-dusted orange wedge.*

Put the Frangelico into a shot glass, then add the vodka. Decorate with the sugared orange wedge. Drink the shot in one gulp, then eat the orange.

1 teaspoon Frangelico hazelnut liqueur
25 ml (1 fl oz) chilled Stolichnaya Razberi vodka
orange wedge dusted with sugar

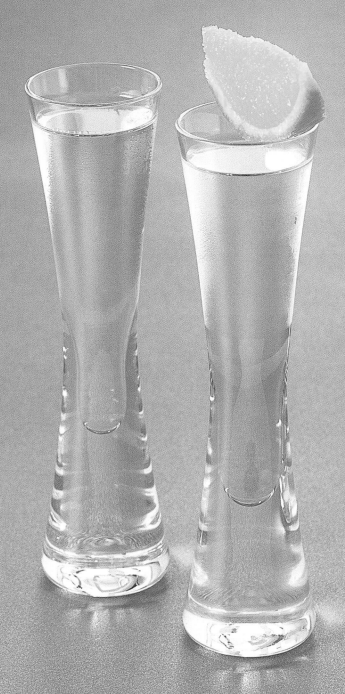

175

Index of Drinks

Acknowledgements

Executive Editor: Sarah Ford
Executive Art Editor: Geoff Fennell
Editor: Katy Denny

Picture Librarian: Jennifer Veall
Production Assistant: Sam Coleman
Special photography: Stephen Conroy